Harry N. Abrams, Inc., Publishers

Peter Lord & Brian Sibley
Foreword by Nick Park

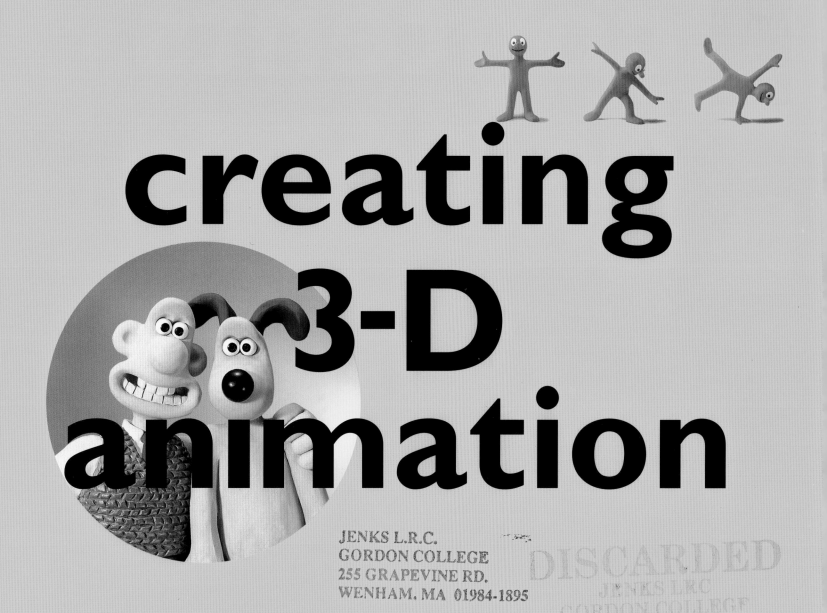

creating 3-D animation

The Aardman Book of Filmmaking

contents

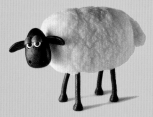

foreword Nick Park

Gromit reacts in terror at his first sighting of the mysterious Techno Trousers in *The Wrong Trousers* (1993), directed by Nick Park.

I wish this book had been written in the Seventies when I was a teenager and started experimenting with animation and making my first movies. I did not meet another animator, or even anyone with a vague knowledge of the technique, for years. My early experience in animation was therefore a solitary one; a case of guesswork and trial and error. I felt that everyone else must be 'doing it right', and there must be something very obvious that everyone else knew about that I was not doing. I scoured old library books and movie magazines for any scraps of information, but found very little.

Later I met Peter Lord and David Sproxton whose work I had long admired. Through them and Aardman Animations I met more of our species, and was surprised to find that they had all felt similarly isolated and had worked through experimentation either at college or on the kitchen table.

This book is an inspiration that provides insights into a world that can seem mysterious and out of reach for the aspiring animator. It is also a thoroughly good nose-around the processes of traditional 3-D animation for those enthusiasts who like to know about these things. This is the book that I always wanted to read but could not ... because it had not been written.

introduction   Peter Lord

Peter Lord with his character Adam. Released in 1991, *Adam* won Aardman an Oscar® nomination.

I began animating as a hobby, when I was a teenager, almost thirty years ago. And though it has now become my career, it has never stopped being a hobby. Other boys of my age were spending their leisure time building model aircraft, or recording train numbers, or sitting on river banks awaiting the appearance of fish. But Fate led me to animation. Fate in the shape of my best friend's Dad, who owned a cine camera.

I met Dave Sproxton, my partner at Aardman, when we were both twelve. We sat at adjoining desks at Woking Grammar School for Boys. His father worked for the BBC as a producer of religious programmes and was also a keen photographer. Like many a producer in those days, and probably to the despair of the Film Union, Vernon Sproxton was not averse to shooting some of his own material if he could get away with it. So he owned a cine camera, a clockwork 16mm Bolex, which was the key factor in our decision to become animators. Along with access to the camera, Dave picked up his father's enthusiasm for photography and an understanding of how films are made. It is significant that Nick Park grew up in a similar environment. His father was a professional photographer who had also dabbled in film-making. He had even done a little bit of animation. So in Nick's family too there was always a cine camera about the place. In both households, film-making was made to seem possible and accessible, even normal.

So we had access to the camera; and one rainy day, probably encouraged by his father, Dave and I experimented with animation. In the great tradition of British amateurism our first film was made on the kitchen table. Only later, after we had served our apprenticeship, did we advance to the spare room. The camera was mounted on a developing stand pointing straight downwards at the table, and our first piece of animation was achieved by drawing a chalk figure on a blackboard, shooting a frame, then rubbing out part of the figure, redrawing it in a new position and shooting another frame. And so on. At the time it seemed painstaking, but compared to some of our subsequent experiences in animation, that first film was a high-speed, spontaneous affair.

We did not launch into animation entirely unprepared. We had seen documentaries about the world of cartoons, and heard how Disney and Hanna Barbera made films with thousands of separate drawings on acetate sheets, but we had no access to the techniques or the materials to shoot this sort of 'traditional' animation. We made up the chalk technique quite independently, to suit our circumstances, though I now know that like so much else in the world of animation it had all been done before - much of it ninety years ago or more!

The original Aardman, a cel sequence featuring an inept figure with a costume based on Superman.

In a matter of hours we became bored with chalk animation, and tried a different technique: cut-outs. We cut pictures out of magazines, crudely cutting off their limbs so they could be animated as separate elements. We had discovered one of the quicker and simpler forms of animation. Our first 'film' consisted of several experiments like this. It was simply a string of animated events, lasting for a couple of minutes. We had no story to tell, no ideas to convey, it was strictly stream of consciousness. We called it *Trash* - not knowing that Andy Warhol had already used the name. It took only a couple of days to complete - although at the time that seemed a pretty mammoth effort - and for the first but not the last time we observed that animation was a slow process. When the developed film came back from the laboratory, we showed it in the living room to our assembled families, with a record on the hi-fi as an accompaniment. And we loved it. We thought it was great. We experienced that sense of magic which happily you never lose, and which I believe is unique to animation. The day-to-day business of animation is usually slow, repetitive and painstaking - and seldom particularly funny. But when it is all over, when the performance is finished, and the hard work mostly forgotten, then you see the result and bingo! - it's alive!

We followed *Trash* with a film called *Godzilla*. Naturally it had no giant lizards in it. It was a similar mix of techniques: cut-outs, chalky, swirly transformations which used the properties of chalk to blur and soften and drag out a line, and a couple of 3-D objects, like toy cars, thrown in for good measure. Though I have not seen either film for twenty years, I assume it was an improvement on *Trash*. When you are just starting out in animation, you learn really fast. Every new completed piece is a revelation. Only when your film is returned from the lab can you see what you have done, for better or worse. Only then can you find out how bad your timing is, how clumsily your drawings move, how insignificant one-twelfth of a second can be.

Shortly after this, Dave's Dad arranged for us to show our work to a producer at the BBC. Patrick Dowling produced the 'Vision On' series, which was

The studio during the early years - when the entire modelmaking department was confined to a single table.

**'Cracking toast, Gromit!'
Wallace and Gromit at the
breakfast table in *A Grand
Day Out* (1989).**

specifically designed for deaf children. It was a great programme - imaginative, brave, technically innovative and stimulating for those with hearing as well as the deaf because it presented visual information in an intelligent and surprising way. The outcome of our first meeting was that PD, as we called him - everyone knew that TV execs were known by their initials - gave us a 100ft roll of film to experiment with. In the late 1960s this precious roll of unexposed negative probably represented the BBC's total investment in new animation talent.

We filled that roll with tests and experiments - some chalk animation, a cel sequence (the original Aardman film), some pixillation (where human beings are treated as animation puppets), and a couple of sequences where we experimented with Plasticine (modelling clay). In one of these, we made a low-relief Plasticine model of a cottage - a crude, childlike thing, I recall. As before, the camera was directly above, looking down on to the model. Under the camera it metamorphosed, as only Plasticine can, into a low-relief model of an elephant. Not the world's greatest storyline, I agree. The BBC showed no inclination to buy this piece, or to commission more, but for me a seed was sown. I had tried this new malleable medium and found it strangely attractive. It took another couple of years for the technique and the storylines to evolve, but our animation future was going to be in three dimensions.

In fact what the BBC did buy was the Aardman sequence. It was a piece of conventional cel animation, and I remember it as the most 'professional' piece on the roll. Aardman is a character that I originally drew in a strip cartoon. He

11

Today the Aardman studio plays host to a growing number of talented film-makers. Here Jeff Newitt acts out the facial expressions of his character while animating him for *Loves Me ... Loves Me Not* (1992).

was based on Superman - in costume, at any rate - with a jutting chin, a cape and a large letter 'A' on his chest. He became the star of our first cel animation, though we left the letter 'A' off his chest, because it took too long to draw.

In his first animated appearance Aardman is walking past, as I recall, a background of brown wrapping paper. He has a goofy walk: legs bent, leaning well back, his arms not swinging but hanging straight by his sides. As he walks, he approaches a cartoon 'hole' - the classic black ellipse on the ground. He stops, sticks out a foot and taps the ellipse. It seems solid. He walks on, right over the 'hole', quite unharmed. One step later, he falls through the ground, down an invisible hole. After a pause, his hand emerges from the ground, feels around, finds the ellipse and pulls it over himself. Then he climbs out and walks off.

That may not be a gripping read, but it was good enough to get bought - and for £15 or so. This was the moment when, faced with a 'purchased programme' agreement and a cheque from the BBC, we opened a bank account in the name of Aardman Animations. I remember discussing the merits of 'Dave and Pete Productions' and numerous other possibilities, but Aardman it was.

Two schoolboys picked a name, little dreaming that it would hang around so long. Now, all those years later, the name no longer stands for a couple of enthusiastic schoolboy film-makers; now we are a company running our own film studio. But the impulse that drives us is still the same. We want to make films, though the reasons why have evolved over the years. Initially, it was terribly simple: two young men making short animated films to amuse themselves, for the pleasure of creation, for the pleasure of communication, to show off, to do something a little different, to get a laugh, to affect people we had never met. Later, as Aardman got bigger and more established, we discovered that we were not just individuals whistling in the dark but part of a scattered and formless community of film-makers in Britain and worldwide.

Then the approval of our peers became important. Suddenly a film was more than just a story told for a few friends, or broadcast to a large unresponsive audience. It became like a public statement, or a brick in the wall of something much larger and oddly noble: 'The World of Animation'. Later on the game changed again as we started to employ people, who made their own films which did not come from Dave and me but were Aardman films. Nick Park is the most famous of the film-makers who have joined us in this way. Then the source of pleasure changed slightly. From being entirely selfish, it became broader: from look-at-me to look-at-us. It was rather like becoming a parent. Before you become a parent, life is more or less selfish. Then, when you have kids, you start to live through them to some extent - for good or ill - enjoying their triumphs and sharing their defeats.

Scene from Peter Lord's medieval fantasy *Wat's Pig* (1996).

When we were just a two-man partnership life, or at any rate business, was simple. But now we are a company and companies operate to a different logic and end up with a different agenda, viz to make money. Of course, it is a good idea for companies to be profitable, but if that is the reason you are in the business of animation, I do not believe you will ever make the best films. Aardman does make money, happily, but it is not what interests or motivates us. It is certainly not why we make films.

The big pleasure for me at this stage in Aardman's evolution is the feeling I sometimes get - not every day, it is true - of being in a community of artists. I love being among dozens of creative people, under one roof, generating ideas, discussing them, interacting, being influenced and affected by each other. The studios too are an exciting place, the product of twenty years of growth and change. Ever since the old days of the kitchen table, we have steadily invested in people and equipment; and as we have met other specialists in our tiny field we have learnt new techniques, tricks and practices which have changed our way of working. Some of the ways we work are standard film-industry practice, some we have learned from other animation studios, some are derived from the theatre and many have simply evolved on site. Technology, culture and working practice have slowly accumulated like a coral reef, or like a junk pile, if you prefer. All that knowledge has been built up by trial and error and by word of mouth over the last twenty years. How often we wished in the early days that some predecessor of ours had written a book like this, to pass on the precious information.

the medium Brian Sibley

Steve Box animates the
fleeing Penguin in the
staircase sequence of *The
Wrong Trousers* (1993).

My aim in this section is to provide an independent view of the history of
animated films, covering both drawn (2-D) and model (3-D) animation, and to
set the work of Aardman Animations in the broader context of a way of
making films that began in the 1890s. One of the earliest films that Peter Lord
and Dave Sproxton created for 'Vision On', the BBC television series for deaf
children, shows a human hand flattening and shaping a ball of clay that then
takes on animated life. First a tiny hand and then an arm reach up out of the
clay, then another hand and arm emerge, followed by the head and torso of a
man, who presses down on the edges of his clay prison, trying to haul himself
up and pull himself free. Then the human hand appears again, seizes the man
and wrenches him - fully formed - from the clay. This little being, made from the
very stuff of the earth itself, looks towards his creator, sits down and assumes
the position of The Thinker ...

The creation myth is very old and is found, with variations, in many different
cultures and faiths. As a symbolic picture, explaining not just the origin of man
but also the source of man's creativity, it has provided a recurrent image for
artists down the centuries and, in particular, for the work of the three-
dimensional animator. Peter Lord, for example, returned to the idea in his
1991 Oscar-nominated film *Adam*, in which the relationship between an
animator and his clay became an amusing analogy for the relationship between
God and Man.

But first things first: what is 3-D animation? Most forms of animated film-making
achieve their effect through essentially flat images either drawn on cels
(transparent sheets which can be overlaid on background paintings and then
photographed), or possibly painted on glass or directly on to the film. A three-
dimensional animator, however, works with articulated puppets or with models
built around a metal, moveable 'skeleton' called an armature, and made of
Plasticine (modelling clay), fabric or latex. Occasionally, the 3-D animator will
work with cut-outs, and he often uses his skills to give animated life to a bizarre
range of inanimate objects from a bra to a burger.

All film, of course, is essentially an optical illusion, a trick of the eye, known as
'persistence of vision'. The human eye retains an image for a fraction of a
second after seeing it. Therefore, if - in that small time-space - an image can be
substituted by another, slightly different, image then movement appears to
occur. What you are really seeing when you look at a cinema screen is not a
moving picture but a series of *still pictures* shown in such rapid succession - at
24 frames every second - that your eye is deceived.

Capturing the dynamics of action: a Greek image of chariot racing from the 6th century BC.

The essential difference between live-action and animated film-making is that the live-action camera captures a scene moving in real time, automatically 'freezing' it into separate still pictures, which can then be projected on to a screen. For the animated film-maker, however, nothing exists to be filmed until it is created and put in front of the camera. Using drawings, models or, increasingly nowadays, computer imagery, the animator creates every single frame of film from scratch. In a live-action film, there is nothing hidden between one frame and the next, whereas the space between every frame of an animated film represents a complex series of creative actions which, if the film is well made, will be undetectable to the audience.

Not only must characters and settings be designed, but decisions must also be taken about what movement will be involved in a scene and the kind of shot - perhaps a close-up or a long-shot - that will be used. So, whilst animation is a highly creative medium, it is weighed down by time-consuming processes which require the successful animator to have vision, vast quantities of patience and a sustained belief in the film that is being made.

There is also a major difference between drawn and model animation, as Peter Lord explains: 'Drawn animation is a process that develops in a very controlled, measurable way. When your character is walking (or jumping or flying) from A to B, you start by drawing position A and position B, the key positions, and then you systematically draw all the positions in between - the animation. But in puppet animation, when you set off from position A you do not know where B is, because you have not got there yet (like real life, come to think of it). So every single stage of a movement is an experiment, or even an adventure. You have this idea of where you are heading, but no certainty of getting there ...'

The desire to animate is as old as art itself. The early man who drew pictures on his cave wall depicting spear-waving hunters in pursuit of a wild boar attempted to convey the illusion of movement by showing the beast with multiple legs. The vases of ancient Greece with their gods and heroes, and the friezes of Rome with their battling warriors and galloping steeds, also sought to capture, in static images, the dynamics of action. Stories of pictures that came to life can be found in folklore and fairy-tale, but it was not until the 19th century - in the years leading up to the invention of the motion picture - that animated pictures became a real possibility.

Among the many pioneers in Europe and America who explored ways of capturing images of real life, and attempted to analyse and replicate movement, were Britain's William Henry Fox Talbot, who devised a photographic method for recording the images of the 'camera obscura', and English-born American, Eadweard Muybridge, who, in 1872, began producing a series of studies of human and animal life, photographed in front of a plain, calibrated backdrop. The photographs, shot every few seconds, revealed what the human eye cannot register: the true complexity involved in the mechanics of physical locomotion.

Muybridge's baseball hitter, who served as a model for the animated sequence shown on pages 138-139.

A photographic sequence by Eadweard Muybridge, whose 19th-century experiments have been of priceless help to later generations of animators.

In 1880, Muybridge conducted one of his most sophisticated experiments when he photographed a running horse using 24 still cameras set up alongside a race track and triggered by a series of trip-wires. Muybridge's photographs of horses, dogs and the naked human form would become an indispensable aid to later generations of animators. Indeed, while Peter Lord was working on some of the models shown in this book, such as the baseball player on pages 138-139, Muybridge's book was a constant source of reference.

Experimentation with photographic and optical techniques led to various devices such as the Stereoscope, which used two slightly different photographic images to create the illusion of 3-D pictures, and sophisticated magic-lantern slides on which parts of the picture could be made to move: a ship tossing on a stormy sea, a rat running into the open mouth of a sleeping man.

The Phenakistiscope, invented in 1832 by Joseph Plateau. When the picture disc is spun, a viewer looking through the slots sees continuous movement. In other versions the slots and pictures are combined on a single disc, and viewed in conjunction with a mirror.

There were also a number of popular optical toys, designed to recreate the illusion of life. The earliest, and simplest, devised in 1825 by Dr John Ayrton Paris, was the Thaumatrope: a disc of card with a picture of a bird on one side and a bird-cage on the other. Strings attached to either side of the disc were twisted tight and held taut; then, when the tension on the strings was released, the disc spun so fast that the bird appeared to be inside the bird-cage.

Seven years later, Joseph Plateau, a physicist from Belgium, invented the Phenakistiscope, a disc fixed to a handle (rather like a child's windmill toy) so that it could spin freely. Around its perimeter the disc had a series of drawn figures in various stages of movement, separated by slots. The disc was held up to a mirror and spun, while the viewer looked through the slots and saw - reflected in the mirror - a running horse, a leaping acrobat or some other moving miracle.

William George Horner of Britain was the first to attempt to create moving images for more than one viewer. He devised the Zoetrope, in which spectators looked through slots in a fast-moving drum at a continuous strip of drawings arranged around the inside. The speed with which the drum revolved blurred the slots into a 'window' and gave life to the static pictures. For variety, the strips of drawings could be changed, but the sequences were limited and repetitious - a dog jumping through a hoop, or a clown's nose endlessly growing and shrinking.

The Praxinoscope, a drum viewer. The images on the perimeter of the drum are reflected in a mirror as they flash past the viewer's eyes.

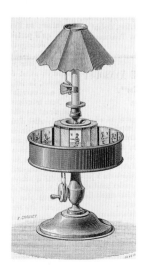

It was due to a visionary Frenchman, Emile Reynaud, that the evolution of the animated film took two major steps forward. The first of these, invented in 1877, was the Praxinoscope, a sophisticated development of the Zoetrope, which enabled viewers to watch the moving pictures as they turned past the eye on a rotating drum.

Reynaud, who was a painter of lantern-slides, spent the next fifteen years improving his device until he found a method of combining the illusion created by the Zoetrope with the projected images seen at the magic-lantern show. The Théâtre Praxinoscope, as it was called, used light and mirrors to show a limited cycle of moving figures against a projected background on what looked like the stage of a toy theatre. Reynaud then further refined his device into the Théâtre Optique, first demonstrated at the Musée Grevin, Paris, in 1892. This elaborate machine simultaneously projected 'moving pictures' and backgrounds on to the same screen. The shows, entitled 'Pantomimes Lumineuses', were not limited to the short cycles of action seen on a Praxinoscope but lasted up to fifteen minutes and comprised some 500 pictures on a transparent strip of gelatin. Although the mechanism had to be turned by hand (a laborious process for the operator), Reynaud's equipment anticipated various cinematic devices including the film-spool and sprocket-holes for moving the pictures on while, at the same time, keeping them in focus. Interestingly, Reynaud used drawings rather than photographic images, and every subsequent animated film using line animation - from Felix the Cat and Mickey Mouse to the Rugrats and the Simpsons - is a successor to the moving pictures that he created.

Reynaud's 'films' were simple - sometimes mildly saucy - tales mainly concerned with love and rivalry: a young lady at a seaside resort goes into a beach hut to change into her bathing costume, unaware that a peeping tom is watching her through the door. The cad is eventually given the boot by a young man who is then rewarded for his gallantry by being allowed to accompany the young lady on a swim. Audiences were amazed and delighted by these moving drawings, but rapid developments quickly provided new entertainments that were to upstage Reynaud's Théâtre Optique.

Experiments by Etienne-Jules Marey in France, Thomas Edison in America and William Friese-Greene and Mortimer Evans in Britain resulted in coin-in-the-slot 'box-projectors' showing acrobatics, ballet and boxing matches, slapstick

Emile Reynaud and his Théâtre Optique, which projected 'moving pictures' and backgrounds on to the same screen.

The rocket lands on the eye of the Moon, from Georges Méliès's fantasy film *Voyage to the Moon* (1902). Many of the visual tricks employed in this film were achieved by stopping the film, altering the image and photographing the new scene. This later became one of the basic techniques of 3-D animation films.

comedy routines or saucy fan dancers. The popularity of such entertainments was eventually eclipsed by the invention of a device that was to change the culture of the world for ever - the Cinématographe.

It was in 1895, just three years after Emile Reynaud showed his Théâtre Optique, that two French brothers, Auguste and Louis Lumière, presented the first authentic demonstration of what we now think of as cinema. There was nothing particularly sophisticated about the Lumières' first films - workers leaving a factory, a baby being spoon-fed, a train entering a station - but to those early audiences they were nothing short of miraculous. Indeed, when the railway engine rushed towards the camera, billowing clouds of smoke and steam, some patrons were so startled by the realism that they fled the theatre before the engine could run them down!

Emile Reynaud's presentations of moving drawings had been superseded. The Lumière brothers were offering audiences not characters from a toy-theatre, but images of real people. However, since the appeal of mere novelty tends to be short-lived, the time soon came when audiences ceased to be astonished at the moving picture's ability to hold a mirror up to life and began to demand stories. The fledgling film-makers responded not just with dramas, comedies and romances but also with fantasies. And there was one fantasy film-maker in particular who made a discovery of vital importance to the technique of film animation.

The films of Georges Méliès grew out of his childhood love of marionettes and toy theatres combined with an adult fascination with conjuring. Describing himself as 'a great amateur of the magical art', Méliès was an accomplished stage-illusionist who saw the new medium of cinema as a natural extension of his magical arts with their transformations, metamorphoses and mysterious appearances and disappearances. The sources for his fantastical films were fairy stories, popular tales and the science-fiction sagas of fellow-Frenchman Jules Verne. He also recreated various classics of magic in which the conventional skills of the magician were replaced by trick photography.

Curiously, the technique enabling Méliès to transform a girl into a butterfly, or make a woman vanish and replace her with a skeleton, was discovered by accident: 'The camera I was using in the beginning (a rudimentary affair in which the film would tear or would often refuse to move) produced an unexpected effect one day [in 1896] when I was photographing very prosaically the Place de l'Opéra. It took a minute to release the film and get the camera going again. During this minute, the people, buses and vehicles had, of course, moved. Projecting the film, having joined the break, I suddenly saw a Madeleine-Bastille omnibus changed into a hearse and men into women. The trick of substitution, called stop action, was discovered, and two days later I made the first metamorphoses of men into women and the first sudden disappearances which had a big success ...'

Although this camera trick had first been used a year earlier in America to create a compelling illusion in the Edison Kinetoscope film, *The Execution of Mary Queen of Scots* (in which, just before the executioner's axe fell, a dummy was substituted for the actress playing the Queen), Méliès was unquestionably the first European film-maker to discover this technique independently. He then use it to great effect.

Stop action (or stop motion) enabled Méliès to create astonishing visual illusions in such trick-film masterpieces as *Voyage to the Moon* (1902), and it subsequently became the standard technique by which, over the decades, many cinema special effects were achieved. 'I do not hesitate to say,' wrote Méliès in 1907, 'that in cinematography it is today possible to realise the most impossible and the most improbable things.' Whilst the basic film technique of animation is universal - film an image, stop the camera, alter the image, film it, stop the camera and alter the image again - the animated film has employed a diversity

Chalk animation by J Stuart
Blackton in *Humorous Phases
of Funny Faces* (1906).
Blackton drew his image on
a blackboard, photographed
it, then erased it, or at least
took out the 'moving' part,
then drew in the next phase.

of media with which to create its illusions of life.
The most popular has been drawn animation,
probably because of the important link between
storytelling and illustration, the heritage of
cartoonists and caricaturists and the visual impact
of graphic design in advertising.

The history of line animation is fascinating but, in
this book, must be briefly told. In 1906, J Stuart
Blackton, a Briton who settled in America and who was to make trick-films with
various media (including, as we shall see, puppets and clay models), produced a
film entitled *Humorous Phases of Funny Faces,* inspired by a then-popular stage
entertainment. One of the speciality acts seen at turn-of-the-century vaudeville
shows was the 'Lightning Sketch' artist who created rapid pictures and portraits,
sometimes undergoing a comic metamorphosis. Blackton recreated this effect
on film with faces drawn on a chalkboard which were then brought to life with
amusing results, as when smoke from a gentleman's cigar billows across the
smiling face of a lady and leaves her scowling. Blackton's process of drawing a
picture, photographing it, rubbing part of it out and then redrawing it was the
most basic use of the stop-motion technique.

A similar process was used, in 1908, by the Parisian caricaturist and film-maker
Emile Cohl in *Fantasmagorie.* The adventures of a little clown, drawn as a
rudimentary stick figure, used some two thousand drawings and ran for under
two minutes. What made *Fantasmagorie* memorable was the bizarre, dreamlike
transformations: a champagne bottle changing into a pineapple which then
becomes a tree, while an elephant turns into a house. There were many artists
who advanced animation such as the brilliant American cartoonist, Winsor
McCay, whose comic newspaper strip 'Little Nemo in Slumberland' (which
frequently had the appearance of being a series of film frames) became an
animated picture in 1911 and was followed, three years later, by *Gertie the
Trained Dinosaur.* This interactive entertainment allowed the real Winsor McCay
to 'converse' with the on-screen Gertie. At the end of the show, McCay would
walk off-stage and reappear as a diminutive animated figure in his own cartoon.

Raoul Barre, whose film series 'The Animated Grouch Chasers' featured a
caricature album that came to life, was responsible for several significant
technical developments such as registration holes in animation paper, to stop
the drawings from wobbling when filmed. Barre also devised a simple method
for cutting down the time-consuming process in which not just the characters
but also the backgrounds had to be redrawn for every single frame of film.
Barre's solution was to draw a single background picture and then animate on

pieces of paper that had been carefully cut so as not to obscure the setting.

It was JR Bray (creator of the comic character Colonel Heeza Liar) who came up with the idea of drawing the backgrounds on sheets of celluloid and placing them on top of the animation drawings. This served until Earl Hurd refined the process by animating his characters on sheets of celluloid that were positioned over painted backgrounds. This technique, pioneered in Hurd's 'Bobby Bump' series, remained (until the recent introduction of computer technology) the standard procedure throughout the industry.

The scene was now set for the emerging talents of a group of artists who would dominate the early years of film animation. They included Pat Sullivan (creator of Felix the Cat) and his collaborator Otto Mesmer; Dave Fleischer (responsible for the 'Out of the Inkwell' series); Paul Terry ('Aesop's Fables'); Walter Lantz (Dinky Doodle and, later, Woody Woodpecker), and the man who created Mickey Mouse, introduced sound and then colour to the animated film, pioneered feature animation and whose name eventually became a synonym for the cartoon film - Walt Disney.

The development of three-dimensional animation is less easily charted since it employed two distinct techniques - one using puppets, the other clay models - each of which went through a particular evolutionary process. In outlining the history of these two traditions, it should be understood that many of the animators whose films will be discussed worked in more than one medium.

Scene from *Gertie the Trained Dinosaur* (1914) by Winsor McCay, an interactive show in which the artist appeared live on stage and as an animated character in the film.

One such was J Stuart Blackton who, with his partner Albert E Smith, had used stop-motion photography to create startling effects in his 1907 live-action film *The Haunted Hotel* and, the following year, produced what is claimed as the first stop-motion puppet film, *The Humpty Dumpty Circus*. This film, now lost, used jointed wood toys of animals and circus performers belonging to Smith's daughter, which were posed and then photographed. Looking back, years later, on the making of this film, Smith recalled: 'It was a tedious process in as much as the movement could be achieved only by photographing separately each position. I suggested we obtain a patent on the process. Blackton felt it wasn't important enough. However, others quickly borrowed the technique, improving upon it greatly.'

A rival claimant for having made the first puppet animated film is the British film-maker Arthur

Melbourne Cooper. Among Cooper's earliest experiments with stop-motion photography was *Matches: An Appeal*, a film of 'moving matchsticks' made in 1899 for the match manufacturer Bryant & May, and probably the world's first animated commercial. For his entertainment films, Arthur Cooper looked for inspiration to the nursery toy cupboard, producing such titles as *Noah's Ark* (1906) and *Dreams of Toyland* (1908), in which a child is given various toys, including a teddy bear and a little wooden horse, and then falls asleep and dreams that the toys come to life. Although Cooper's method of filming outdoors with sunlight had its drawbacks - the combination of the stop-motion process and the earth's rotation produced strange, flickering shadows - he went on to make other successful films on similar themes, including *Cinderella* and *Wooden Athletes* (both 1912) and *The Toymaker's Dream* (1913).

The 'toys come to life' was a recurrent scenario with early animators partly because toys (particularly ones with jointed limbs) made good actors and because the idea connected with a strong European literary tradition of stories about living toys. A typical example - which also incorporated the popular dream device - is Italian film-maker Giovanni Pastrone's film *The War and the Dream of Momi* (1913), in which an old man tells his young grandson, Momi, tales of war. Falling asleep, Momi dreams of a dramatic battle between puppets, during which he gets spiked by one of the soldier's bayonets. The boy wakes to discover that the weapon was in fact only a rose-thorn.

Children's dreams and animated toys figure prominently in the films of the pioneering puppet animator, Ladislaw Starewich. In *The Magic Clock* (1928), automata figures of kings, princesses, knights and dragons, decorating a fantastical clock, come alive and embark on an adventure which is not

A child's toys come to life in *Dreams of Toyland* (1908) by Arthur Melbourne Cooper.

controlled by clockwork. Another, *Love in Black and White* (1927), concerns an accident-prone travelling showman whose puppet performers include likenesses of Hollywood stars Tom Mix, Mary Pickford and Charlie Chaplin.

Born to a Polish-Lithuanian family in 1882, Starewich had a passion for drawing and sculpture and was interested in photography, magic lanterns and early attempts at film animation such as Emile Cohl's 1908 film *The Animated Matches*, which he saw when it was screened in Russia. Starewich was also fascinated by entomology and it was while studying (and attempting to photograph) insect life that he decided to adopt the stop-motion technique used in Emil Cohl's film: 'In the mating season, beetles

Charlie Chaplin is one of several Hollywood-inspired performers in *Love in Black and White* (1927) by Ladislaw Starewich, the pioneering puppet animator.

fight. Their jaws remind one of deers' horns. I wished to film them but, since their fighting is nocturnal, the light I used would freeze them into total immobility. By using embalmed beetles, I reconstructed the different phases of that fight, frame by frame, with progressive changes; more than five hundred frames for thirty seconds of projection. The results surpassed my hopes: *Lucanus Cervus* (1910, 10 metres long), the first three-dimensional animated film ...'

Within a year, Starewich had produced a more ambitious film. Entitled *The Beautiful Leukanida*, it was 250 metres long and told how the beautiful beetle, Elena, became the subject of a duel between two rival insect suitors. The film was widely acclaimed and audiences were astonished, and mystified, by Starewich's photography. Many people found the film totally inexplicable, and journalists in London confidently revealed that Starewich had filmed living insects that had been carefully trained by a Russian scientist! It is small wonder that such theories were put forward, since Starewich's animation of his spindly-limbed characters was extraordinarily accomplished.

Starewich's cast of insect characters appeared in a series of modern fables, among them *The Cameraman's Revenge* (1911) which featured such tiny miracles as a grasshopper on a bicycle and a dragonfly ballet dancer. Perhaps because they take the viewer into a secret world, these films are as amusing and ingenious as when they were made eighty years ago. In 1919, Starewich moved to Paris, adopted a French spelling of his name - Ladislas Starevitch - and, for a time, occupied a studio formerly used by Georges Méliès.

25

The country lad and the sophisticated urbanite in one of Ladislaw Starewich's animal fables, _Town Rat, Country Rat_ (1926).

Recognising that the characters in his insect films were limited by their lack of facial expressions, Starewich began making puppets of mammal characters for such films as _Town Rat, Country Rat_ (1926) and his elaborate feature-length film, _The Tale of the Fox_, which he began working on in 1925 and completed five years later, but which was not released until 1938.

The Tale of the Fox, an episodic story based on the fables of La Fontaine, features the exploits of a cunning Fox who is forever tricking the other animals - particularly a slow-witted Wolf. There is also a Lion King and his Lioness Queen as well as a wily Badger who acts as defence counsel when charges are brought against the Fox by assorted chickens, ravens, and rabbits. Although the animals in Starewich's films wear human clothes, in the style of a thousand book illustrations, they seem more like human characters in animal masks. Starewich crams every scene with characters and activity: frogs sing, mice dance and birds flutter among the trees. The physical animation is exceptional: when the fox schemes, his eyes narrow and his lip curls in a sinister sneer, and when a feline troubadour serenades the Queen, Her Majesty closes her eyes in ecstasy and we see the royal breast heaving with emotion.

In _The Mascot_ (1934), Starewich returned to toys with a live-action story about a poor toy-maker whose daughter is feverish and asking for the impossible - a cool, juicy orange. Duffy, a toy puppy-dog, hears and notes her request. The following day, the toys stage an escape from the van that is taking them to market and Duffy sets off to find an orange. Duffy succeeds in his mission, but among his adventures in the real world - represented by intercutting with live-action - is a nightmarish episode in which he finds himself in a sinister backstreet underworld ruled by a Devil doll and inhabited by goblins, insects and reptiles, anthropomorphic turnips, carrots and hair-brushes, a motheaten stuffed monkey, a gruesome mummified character with trailing bandages and the animated skeletons of chickens and fish. At the conclusion of this scary sequence, the Devil bursts open and collapses into a heap of sawdust.

An eccentric restaging of Lewis Carroll's mad tea-party in Jan Svankmajer's _Alice_ (1987).

26

Homunculus figure in Jan Svankmajer's treatment of Faust (1994). Svankmajer achieves haunting effects in his films with his mixtures of live action and animation.

In its more bizarre and beastly moments, *The Mascot* foreshadows the films, three decades later, of Czech animator Jan Svankmajer. In his film *Alice* (1987), a skeletal fish and a small animal skull with doll's eyes and tiny human legs travel in a coach pulled by white cockerels with skulls instead of heads.

From his first film, *The Last Trick* (1964), Svankmajer brought to the cinema the theatrical skills of masks and puppets, combining them with film animation techniques using clay, models, cut-outs and inanimate objects conjured into life with a sharply focused surreal imagination that is endlessly startling. Svankmajer's films play on universal phobias: dark cellars and empty houses; dead things - such as an ox's tongue - that look uncomfortably human; and dangerous things such as nails, scissors and broken glass. His subject matter flies in the face of social taboos, linking food, death and sex, pain and pleasure in shocking, unforgettable imagery.

Film titles such as *Jabberwocky* (1971), *The Fall of the House of Usher* (1981) and

The Brothers Quay, Stephen and Timothy, on the set of *Street of Crocodiles* (1986). The original films of these two Americans bear the influence of both Jan Svankmajer and the Eastern European puppet tradition.

The Pit and the Pendulum (1983) reveal two of the major influences on Svankmajer - Lewis Carroll and Edgar Allan Poe - and reflect his fascination with dream states: those uncertain regions where reality and unreality are excitingly - and often frighteningly - blurred; states of mind where a pile of old shoes, their soles coming adrift from the uppers, become a pack of snapping dogs, or where a stuffed rabbit can sew up a gaping seam to prevent the sawdust from spilling out.

Svankmajer's films often combine animation with live action, as in *Alice* and his other feature *Faust* (1994), but whether pixillating live actors or manipulating china dolls, joints of uncooked meat or, in *Dimensions of Dialogue* (1982), two lumps of deathly-grey clay which form themselves into heads and then eat and regurgitate one another, Svankmajer is an undaunted renegade of animation art.

A compelling animated documentary on Svankmajer's work, *The Cabinet of Jan Svankmajer: Prague's Alchemist of Film,* was made in 1984 by Stephen and Timothy Quay, twin brothers born in Philadelphia, USA, but working primarily in Britain. The Brothers Quay, as they are known, owe much to Svankmajer's inspiration and their films, which include *Nocturna artificialia* (1979) and *Street of Crocodiles* (1986), present a complex vision of a dusty, decaying world where the overpowering feeling is one of claustrophobia and Kafkaesque confusion. For all their originality, the Quay brothers' films acknowledge the Eastern European heritage of puppet film-making, a tradition which itself springs from the long and distinguished heritage of the puppet theatre.

Soldiers parade next to the bound body of their captive, from *The New Gulliver* (1935) by Alexander Ptushko.

That heritage was the motivating force behind many of the earliest puppet films which - although now virtually unknown or seldom seen - were hailed in their day as being innovative cinema. *The New Gulliver* (1935) by the Russian animator, Alexander Ptushko, features another dream story in which a boy falls asleep over a copy of *Gulliver's Travels*. Ptushko's film includes scenes filmed in the camera (as opposed to being created through optical techniques in processing), incorporating a live actor and some 3000 puppets. Ptushko went on to produce a number of feature-length films combining animation and live-action including *The*

Fisherman and the Little Fish (1937) and *The Little Golden Key* (1939), based on a Russian version of *Pinocchio* by Alexander Tolstoi in which an organ-grinder, Papa Karlo, transforms an amazing talking log into a little wooden boy named Buratino.

In 1935, the same year that Ptushko released *The New Gulliver*, the Hungarian-born animator George Pal produced an exquisite film, *The Ship of the Ether*, featuring the voyage of a ship made from blown glass. Pal's earliest films were made in Germany, where he used stop-motion photography to produce an animated commercial for a cigarette company in Cologne: 'They liked it so much that they ordered other films where the cigarettes spoke. So we put little mouths on them - no faces yet, just mouths. And then we put faces on them, and put hats on them, and put arms and legs on them - wire legs with buttons for feet...'

A ship made from blown glass in George Pal's exquisite film *The Ship of the Ether* (1935).

With the rise of Nazism in 1933, Pal moved to Eindhoven in Holland where he produced a series of fairy-tale subjects such as *The Magic Lamp* and *Sinbad the Sailor*. At what was soon the biggest puppet-animation studio in Europe, Pal was making short entertainment films for commercial sponsors such as Phillips Radio, Unilever and Horlicks. Then, in 1939, George Pal moved to America and set up studio in Hollywood where, assisted by some of the finest puppet animators from Europe, he began producing a series of theatrical shorts which he called 'Puppetoons'.

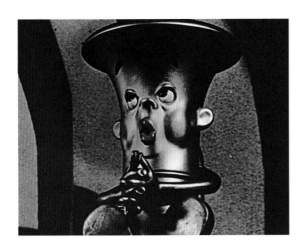

George Pal's musical fantasy *Tubby the Tuba* (1947), using techniques developed in his short puppet films which he called 'Puppetoons'

Pal's early puppets were very basic: heads and hands tended to be wooden balls, bodies were blocks of wood and limbs were made of bendy covered wire. Although they would become more sophisticated, they remained highly stylised with movements that have an almost mechanical precision producing a look not unlike that achieved, decades later, with early computer animation. Pal's films required the use of a great many models or part-models: for a Puppetoon to walk through a scene might require the use of as many as 24 sets of legs, while up to 100 replacement heads could be used for a character in one of his more elaborate films such as *Tubby the Tuba* (1947).

George Pal surrounded by some of the army of puppets he used to film by the substitution method (see also pages 86-87).

Based on a story by Paul Trip and music by George Kleinsinger, *Tubby the Tuba* was a tale about a tuba in an orchestra who (much to the amusement of the other instruments) wanted to play a 'tune' as opposed to just oompah-ing away in the background. With the help of a genial bull-frog, Tubby learns a tune and, in turn, teaches it to the rest of the orchestra. This simple fable about accepting others for what they are (and, indeed, learning to accept yourself) is a good example of Pal's film-making: funny, touching and deftly animated.

Pal was, however, capable of darker visions such as *Tulips Shall Grow* (1942), a powerful anti-Nazi film in which an idyllic picture-book portrayal of Holland - tulips, windmills and a pair of cute, clog-wearing lovers - is suddenly overrun by a marauding army of goose-stepping mechanical men. Made from nuts, bolts and washers, the robotic soldiers carry banners declaring themselves to be the 'Screwballs'. Bombs rain down from metal, bat-shaped planes until the windmills are broken skeletons against a blood-red sky. Only when it rains do the armies finally grind to a halt in a sea of rust.

One of the most popular of Pal's characters was a little black boy named Jasper who appeared in almost twenty films with such titles as *Jasper Goes Fishing* (1943), *Jasper and the Beanstalk* (1945) and *Jasper in a Jam* (1946). Also in 1946 Pal made *John Henry and the Inky Poo* (1946), a powerful little film based on the American folk tale of the black railroad ganger who competed with a track-laying machine called the Inky Poo. John Henry, depicted in a naturalistic style that is far removed from that of the Jasper films, wins his spike-driving contest and, though he dies in the effort, proves that 'there ain't a machine made that can beat a man once a man's got a mind he can beat that machine'.

Scene from Ray Harryhausen's puppet version of the Hansel and Gretel story.

Laurence Harvey as the Shoemaker with George Pal's elves in *The Wonderful World of the Brothers Grimm* (1962).

George Pal's Puppetoons won an affectionate audience in America and a number of model animators who worked on the films went on to successful careers of their own, including Joop Geesink who produced his own series of puppet films under the generic title 'Dollywood', and Ray Harryhausen who, in 1945, began producing a short series of films with fairy-tale subjects.

The first of these films, *Mother Goose Stories*, featured highly detailed sets and charming 'cartoon-style' puppets of Humpty Dumpty, Little Miss Muffet, Old Mother Hubbard and others. Harryhausen then made *Little Red Riding Hood*, *Hansel and Gretel*, *The Story of Rapunzel* and *The Story of King Midas* before concentrating on stop-motion special effects. Harryhausen's fairy-tale films show the skill of an exceptional puppet-maker. His slavering wolves, bald-headed demons and warty-nosed hags foreshadow the fiends and monsters which he was later to create for the live-action cinema.

As for George Pal, he went on to produce and direct a memorable string of science-fiction and fantasy films such as *Destination Moon* (1950), *When Worlds Collide* (1951) and his unforgettable versions of HG Wells's *The War of the Worlds* (1953) and *The Time Machine* (1960). Many of these films

Floating, Chagall-like image of Ariel with Prospero in Stanislav Sokolov's *The Tempest* (1992). This was one of a series of films called 'Shakespeare, the Animated Tales' made as a co-production by S4C/BBC/Christmas Films, Moscow.

Another of Trnka's creative heirs is the Japanese puppet animator Kihachiro Kawamoto. Born in Sedagaya in 1925, Kawamoto saw Jiri Trnka's *The Emperor's Nightingale* and travelled to Europe to study with the Czech film-maker before working in Hungary, Poland, Rumania and Russia and then returning to Japan. Kawamoto's films, which include *Demon* (1972), *A Poet's Life* (1974), *Dojoji* (1976) and *House of Flame* (1979), unite the European approach to puppet film-making with the long tradition of puppetry in Japan which dates back to the Bunraku puppet plays first presented in the 17th century.

Drawing his inspiration from the masks of the Noh drama, Kawamoto's puppets are not only animated with precision, they are also painstakingly made: 'The creation of a single puppet takes ten days. The head requires particular care. First I prepare a plaster mould with which I fashion the head from an agglomerate of Japanese paper, which is then covered with a fine, supple leather and subsequently painted; thus it is light but solid. Eyes, mouth and eyebrows are moveable, and the ears, in plastic, are made from moulds ... Teeth are fashioned from a type of paraffin, the chests from rigid paper; the hands, in supple rubber, are easily moved. For ten minutes of animation, one year of preparation is required.'

Scene from Galina Beda's
***Ruth* (1996), one of the**
'Testament' series made by
S4C/BBC/Christmas Films,
Moscow.

Where some puppet-film animators have followed the aesthetic principles of Jiri Trnka, including Polish-born Yoram Gross, whose *Joseph the Dreamer* (1961) was the first such film to be animated in Israel, others, such as Norway's Ivo Caprino, have returned to the realistic style of Ladislaw Starewich. Caprino's masterpiece, *The Pinchcliffe Grand Prix* (1975), is a fast-paced action-comedy about a remarkable car called 'Il Tempo Gigante', and contains scenes that are literally crowded to overflowing with charming and eccentric characters.

Some of the finest puppet animation in recent years has emerged from a collaboration between the British television company S4C, the BBC and the Moscow-based group of animators, Christmas Films. Three series (using a variety of animation media) have been made: 'Shakespeare, The Animated Tales', 'Operavox' and 'Testament' including, among many fine pieces of animation, Stanislav Sokolov's elemental visualisation of *The Tempest* (1992); Maria Muat's *Twelfth Night* (1992) which captures the romance, confusion and buffoonery of Shakespeare's comedy, and Galina Beda's *Ruth* (1996) which retells the moving Old Testament story of love and loyalty with a precision and delicacy that recalls the work of Trnka.

These films received great acclaim in Britain and America, two countries which - whilst slow to embrace the puppet film - have had a long fascination with automata, marionettes, glove-puppets and ventriloquists' dolls. Unlikely though it may seem, two of the greatest stars in the early days of American radio were ventriloquist Edgar Bergen's dummies Charlie McCarthy and Mortimer Snerd. Similarly, in Britain, Peter Brough and his cheeky companion, Archie Andrews, were hugely successful on both radio and television.

One of the top-rated TV shows in America in the 1950s was that featuring the string-puppet Howdy Doody, while, for a later generation, Jim Henson's glove-puppets achieved national, and then international stardom with 'Sesame Street' and 'The Muppet Show'. In Britain, where puppet plays featuring the characters Punch and Judy have been a centuries-long part of the nation's popular culture, many of the earliest television shows for children featured marionettes. Rather than use expensive and time-consuming stop-motion photography, the puppets were manipulated 'live' before the camera and appeared, strings and all! Nevertheless, characters such as Andy Pandy, Muffin the Mule, The Woodentops

and Bill and Ben, the Flowerpot Men (all between 1950 and 1955) quickly established themselves as children's favourites.

By the end of the 1950s, puppet shows on television were becoming more elaborate with Gerry Anderson's 'The Adventures of Twizzle' and 'Torchy the Battery Boy', both of which featured fantastic child heroes: Twizzle, with endlessly extending arms and legs, and Torchy, a human battery with a light in his hat that had magical properties. Anderson also made a puppet Western series, 'Four Feather Falls', featuring Sheriff Tex Tucker, Rocky his horse and Dusty his dog. This was a revolutionary series which aimed at satisfying the expectations of an increasingly sophisticated audience. New techniques enabled Anderson to manipulate his puppets with extra fine wires that, at 1/5000th of an inch thick, were scarcely visible. A further development, electronically sychronising lip-movements, added a realism not usually associated with puppet characters.

Anderson's pioneering television puppet films continued with 'Supercar' (1961), 'Fireball XL5' (1963), 'Stingray' (1964), and the phenomenally successful 'Thunderbirds' (1965), filmed in what Anderson called 'Supermarionation'. But, despite strong characters, dramatic plots and the endlessly fascinating sci-fi gadgets and gizmos with which the cars, boats and planes were fitted, Anderson's puppets still had strings attached.

Scene from Serge Danot's series 'The Magic Roundabout' which enjoyed a long career on BBC Television from 1965.

One film-maker who found the confidence to cut the strings and turn to stop-motion photography was Gordon Murray who, at the beginning of the Sixties, was producing elaborate puppet plays about the bewigged inhabitants of a Ruritanian principality named Rubovia, but who within only a few years was producing stop-motion films about the small-town dramas in idealised rural communities (represented by model-village settings and characters in 1930s costumes) called 'Camberwick Green' (1966) and 'Trumpton' (1967) .

In 1964, modelmaker Oliver Postgate and writer Peter Firman created one of the earliest stop-motion puppet series on British television with their forest fantasies about the lives of the folk in 'Pogles' Wood'. Postgate and Firman's company - modestly named Smallfilms - went on to produce such series as 'The Clangers' (1969), about a race of small pink knitted creatures (vaguely resembling aardvarks) who lived in holes - covered by dustbin-lids - on a small blue planet; and 'Pingwings', about a race of black-and-white knitted creatures (something like penguins) who lived in a barn on Berrydown Farm.

In France, Serge Danot created 'The Magic Roundabout' (from 1965) with its cast of memorable eccentrics, including a dog that looked like an animated floor mop, a pink cow and a moustachioed character on a spring. This series was greatly loved in France and - thanks to a free-wheeling translation - in Britain, and later inspired a feature-length film, *Dougal and the Blue Cat* (1970). One of Danot's animators was British-born Ivor Wood, who later joined Filmfair, a stop-motion animation studio founded by Graham Clutterbuck and responsible for such series as 'The Wombles' (1973), about a race of shaggy-haired, long-nosed litter-gatherers who live on Wimbledon Common. Ivor Wood went on to create his own enchanting series, 'Postman Pat' (1981), about the daily exploits - and occasional daring adventures - of a genial, bespectacled country postman and Jess, his black-and-white cat.

All these series - regardless of whether their characters were made out of wood, fabric or knitting-wool - had a Trnka-like simplicity of shape and fixed expressions. In contrast, many of the films produced by Cosgrove Hall (a partnership of two British artists, Brian Cosgrove and Mark Hall) have preferred the detailed realism and moving features pioneered by Ladislaw Starewich.

Cosgrove Hall's full-length film of *The Wind in the Willows* (1983), and the series

The characters' mobile features and subtle eye and lip movements were widely praised in the Cosgrove Hall film of *The Wind in the Willows* (1983).

which followed it, featured finely crafted puppets meticulously brought to life with movements which suggest a combination of animal behaviour and human nature ideally suited to Kenneth Grahame's original characters, who sometimes seem to be animals in human clothes and at other times appear more like humans wearing animal masks.

Lou Bunin with a character from his *Alice in Wonderland* (1948), which included live and puppet players.

Working with rubber moulded heads, Cosgrove Hall have shown that it is possible to achieve the most subtle eye and lip movements. However, because latex always has a rubbery look, it is far more suited to modelling animals with skin, such as Toad, than furry creatures like Mole and Rat. Additionally, all moulded rubber puppets run the risk of showing tell-tale traces of the joins on the plaster moulds from which they are made.

Despite these drawbacks, Cosgrove Hall's numerous films - in various animation media - have been extremely successful. Their later puppet film series include a superb three-dimensional recreation of the Toyland home of Enid Blyton's *Noddy* (1992) and *Oakie Doke* (1995) which introduced the title-character - an engaging tree-sprite with an acorn head and oak-leaf 'ears' - who helps the woodland creatures to solve their various

In Tim Burton's *Vincent*, the eponymous hero is a seven-year-old boy who models his life on the movie career of horror star Vincent Price, whose voice is heard on the soundtrack.

problems. In 1991, Cosgrove Hall also made a feature-length puppet film, based on *Truckers*, Terry Pratchett's novel about a diminutive - and fast-diminishing - race of 'Nomes' who survive by travelling the motorways of Britain in 'borrowed' trucks. And, most recently, their sensitivity in creating small, utterly convincing imaginary worlds has been demonstrated in the film versions of Jill Barklem's stories about *Brambley Hedge*. In America, Lou Bunin made a version of *Alice in Wonderland* (1948) which used live and puppet players, and Jules Bass produced a series of Christmas specials, such as *Rudolph the Red Nosed Reindeer* (1964), and a feature-length film, *Mad Monster Party* (1968), in which Dr Frankenstein summons a convention of movie monsters. Apart from these films, however, and the work of George Pal, American puppet animated films have been a rarity. Even the powerful Disney studio only ever flirted with the medium a couple of times with *Noah's Ark* (1959) and *A Symposium on Popular Songs* (1962). Both films were nominated for Academy Awards and featured animated characters made from fabric and assorted household objects including an Arkload of kitchen-utensil animals. Then, in 1982, a young artist at the Disney studio came up with a bizarre idea for a short puppet horror film aimed at children!

Tim Burton's *Vincent* told the story of a strange little boy who modelled his life on the movie career of his idol, the horror star Vincent Price. Burton's stylised puppets - uncomfortably sharp and angular - were animated by Stephen Chiodo and shot in black and white with a lot of atmospheric shadow. The hero's unnatural preferences for the dark, for reading books by Edgar Allan Poe and conducting Frankenstein-like experiments on his dog, were wittily presented and perfectly complemented by the voice of the real Vincent Price on the soundtrack. But, at the time, the film was decidedly not a Disney picture.

Burton made one more attempt to exercise his macabre imagination at the Disney studio with *Frankenweenie* (1984), a live-action pastiche of Universal's *Frankenstein*, after which he left to become a Hollywood legend in his own right with such grotesque films as *Beetlejuice*, *Edward Scissorhands* and the first two of the new dark breed of Batman movies.

While pursuing his live-action film-making career, Tim Burton still had in mind a scenario which he had developed while he was with Disney, but which had never been put into production. Eventually, at what was by now a very different Disney studio, work began on *A Nightmare Before Christmas*. Directed by a talented animator, Henry Selick, Burton's *Nightmare* told the saga of Jack Skellington, the Pumpkin King, who rules the darkly sinister world of Halloween but who would much rather have the job of being Father Christmas. The elaborate film featured 227 puppets - vampires, werewolves, ghosts, gargoyles, mummies and freaks - many of which could be fitted with an extensive range of heads or faces in an animation process that, though superbly executed, was merely a sophisticated version of the methods used, years before, by George Pal.

A Nightmare Before Christmas (1993) was the first stop-motion feature film to receive worldwide distribution. Some of the finest model animators in the world brought the creepy characters eerily to life on elaborate sets with grotesque anthropomorphic buildings, crumbling masonry, rusting railings and dank cobbled streets, all of which were textured to have the look of the scratchy, cross-hatched penwork found in Tim Burton's original drawings.

The mischievous Lock, Shock and Barrel in Tim Burton's *A Nightmare Before Christmas* (1993).

Many of the figures were a triumph of modelmaking and animation, for example the cadaverous Jack - a black-suited figure, all skull and bones - whose arms and legs had no more thickness than a pipe-cleaner, yet who moved with an elegant gracefulness without a hint of a shimmer or a shake.

The popular and critical success of *Nightmare* prompted the Disney studio to make, again under

Harryhausen worked as O'Brien's assistant on a further ape picture, *Mighty Joe Young* (1949), and was responsible for the greater part of the film's animation effects. He also animated O'Brien's dinosaur models in the prehistoric sequences of *The Animal World* (1956) and, in his own right, went on to create some of the most memorable stop-motion monsters in the history of the cinema: *The Beast from 20,000 Fathoms* (1953); the giant octopus in *It Came from Beneath the Sea* (1955); the Ymir, duelling with an elephant in the Colosseum in *20 Million Miles to Earth* (1957), and yet more dinosaurs in *One Million Years BC* (1966) and *The Valley of Gwangi* (1969).

In fantasy films that range from *The 7th Voyage of Sinbad* (1958) to *The Clash of the Titans* (1981), Ray Harryhausen brought to life a troupe of terrifying mythological creatures - sirens, dragons, centaurs, griffins, a two-headed roc and a one-eyed Cyclops. Ray Bradbury once referred to these alarming and alluring creatures of Harryhausen's genius as 'the delicious monsters that moved in his head and out of his fingers and into our eternal dreams'. In what is probably Ray Harryhausen's finest film, *Jason and the Argonauts* (1963), there is a stunning episode in which live-action star Todd Armstrong fights a skeletal army, born from the scattered teeth of a Hydra. It is a breathtaking sequence of screen magic which has inspired many animators, including Aardman's Peter Lord and Dave Sproxton.

Although, in the earliest days of cinema, clay animation had featured prominently, its use declined as a reaction to the increasing sophistication in cel-animation techniques. A curiosity from this transitional period is *Modeling* (1921), a film in the 'Out of the Inkwell' series in which live-action footage showed animator Max Fleischer drawing his cartoon character Ko Ko the clown, who would then embark on some escapade both on, and off, the drawing-board. In one episode, Max's fellow animator, Roland Crandall, is seen sculpting a bust of a gentleman with a grotesquely large nose. The sitter arrives and is not best pleased with the likeness. Meanwhile, on paper, Ko Ko is having fun in a winter landscape, building a snowman who also has a huge nose. To stop Ko Ko's antics, Max throws a lump of real clay on to the line-animated image. The clown throws the clay back, escapes from the drawing and runs amok in the studio. Before being returned to the inkwell, Ko Ko climbs on to the sculpture of the large-nosed gentleman and hides in one of the cavernous nostrils.

Drawing by Ray Harryhausen for one of the animation sequences in *Jason and the Argonauts* (1963).

The on-screen realisation of the battle between Jason (Todd Armstrong) and his skeletal opponents in *Jason and the Argonauts*.

Following the release, in 1927, of Walt Disney's *Steamboat Willie*, the first cartoon with synchronised sound, the public appetite for cel animation left little room for any other medium. Apart from one or two highly stylised experimental films, such as Leonard Tregillus's and Ralph Luce's *No Credit* (1948) and *Proem* (1949), clay animation had all but been abandoned.

The medium was not revived until 1955, when Art Clokey created a character who has been described as 'almost irritating in his utter cuteness', but who became an American institution - Gumby. Art Clokey produced 127 six-minute films featuring Gumby and his little horse, Pokey, each of which was a combination of ingenious animation effects (frequently achieved on a shoestring budget) and scenarios that reflected their creator's strongly held beliefs in fairness, tolerance and goodness. The innocence in Gumby's personality is reflected in his look: an arrangement of geometric shapes making the character easy to construct and animate. Gumby is essentially a flat, upended rectangle of greenish-blue clay, divided at the bottom into two splayed, footless legs.

Characters in one of Will
Vinton's adventurous
advertising films made for
the California Raisin
Advisory Board.

of the title character with his mane of white hair, walrus moustache, twinkling
eyes and ever-present cigar. Will Vinton's *Twain* is an incomparable example of
human animation in a style that subtly combines naturalism with caricature. The
film also contains numerous stunning special effects as when one of the books
in Mark Twain's airborne library snaps open and a river of multi-coloured clay
flows and splashes out. *The Adventures of Mark Twain* received a limited critical
success as did the Disney live-action feature film, *Return to Oz* (1985), to which
Will Vinton contributed amazing animated effects. This sombre, songless sequel
to the happy-go-lucky MGM classic returns Dorothy to a now ruined Emerald
City and, among various scary encounters, she visits the underworld domain of
the Nome King who, in an ingenious Claymation sequence, is gradually
transformed from an animated rockface into the
actor Nicol Williamson.

**The weird and wonderful
vessel in Will Vinton's *The
Adventures of Mark Twain*
(1985), also known as *Comet
Quest*, the first clay animated
feature film.**

In America, Will Vinton's pioneering work has since
been overshadowed by the phenomenal success of
his clever series of advertising films for the
California Raisin Advisory Board. Designed to make
raisins appealing to a young audience, Vinton
created a group of anthropomorphic raisins who
sing and play rock-and-roll music. Beginning with
Marvin Gaye's song, 'I Heard It through the
Grapevine', the series went on to feature the music
of Michael Jackson and Ray Charles, performed by
raisin caricatures of those musicians. Although Will

Morph, with his friend and alter-ego Chas, was an early creation of Peter Lord and Dave Sproxton, and first appeared in the BBC 'Vision On' series in 1976.

Vinton took the art of clay animation to new heights of invention and sophistication, the medium failed successfully to challenge the supremacy of cel animation, particularly with the revival of animation talent at the Disney studio, beginning in 1989 with *The Little Mermaid*.

The present renaissance in clay animation had its origins in 1960s Britain with the work of Peter Lord and Dave Sproxton. Whilst still at school, and then university, Lord and Sproxton began contributing short animated films to a BBC television programme for deaf children called 'Vision On'. They were influenced in their ambition to animate by the films of Ray Harryhausen (especially *Jason and the Argonauts*) and by Terry Gilliam's work for the avant-garde television comedy series, 'Monty Python's Flying Circus'. They also aspired to equal the quality of animation seen in some of the puppet-film series then being shown on British TV, such as 'The Wombles' and 'The Magic Roundabout'. The fact that Serge Danot's 'Roundabout' had also established a large adult following suggested to them that the appeal of animation might not simply be limited to 'kid's stuff'.

Lord and Sproxton eventually focused on developing their skills with Plasticine/clay animation, mainly because nobody else in Britain appeared to be working in the medium (which gave it a saleable uniqueness) and because it offered a flexibility denied to the most sophisticated puppet. An early example of a clay film sequence for 'Vision On' featured a real table with a real plate on which clay food - sausages, peas and potatoes - moved around before merging into what Peter Lord describes as 'a muddy brown quadruped like a bear or a wombat', which then walked off the plate.

The success of these short pieces led to the creation, in 1976, of Morph, the small terracotta man who interacted with the programme's artist Tony Hart, and who had a propensity for 'morphing' into animals, objects or sometimes just a ball of the raw material of which he was made. Viewers responded to Morph's simple shape, friendly features and warm colour; he quickly became a star of the small screen and secured Lord and Sproxton's reputation. His regular appearances on 'Vision On' were followed by a series, 'The Adventures of Morph' (1981-3), in which he was joined by an ever-expanding family of delightful and quirky characters.

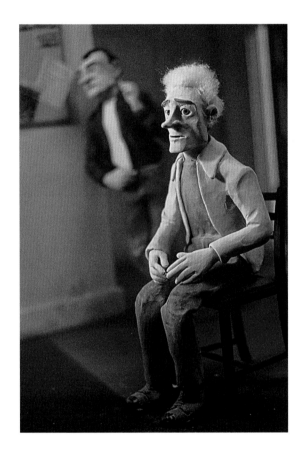

A scene from *On Probation*, one of five ground-breaking films in the Aardman series 'Conversation Pieces' (1982-3). For these films, Peter Lord and Dave Sproxton built their stories around real-life taped interviews, but they themselves never met the people involved.

In 1978, Aardman Animations' work took a quantum leap when they were commissioned to make two short films, called 'Animated Conversations', for late-night screening by BBC Bristol. Taking the skills mastered in animating Morph, Lord and Sproxton applied them to realistic human figures acting out small, intimate dramas based on true-life situations.

The soundtracks for 'Animated Conversations' used voices of 'real people', recorded in various day-to-day situations. For example, in the first film, *Confessions of a Foyer Girl*, two usherettes in a cinema foyer talk about boys and boredom and what they are going to do when they get home from work. The concept of 'Animated Conversations' was developed into a series of five 'Conversation Pieces' (1982-3) for Channel 4, using increasingly sophisticated animation to depict ways in which people succeed - but more often fail - at communication. *On Probation* depicts a group meeting where a tortuous exchange takes place between a young man who needs to visit a member of his family and a probation officer who is trying to negotiate the terms of the visit - with various unhelpful interjections from the other members of the group. The resulting drama is filled with brilliant observation - people tapping pencils, taking off their spectacles, looking edgily at one another - and is ultimately funnier, sadder and far more memorable than if the same small scenario had been presented in live action.

With their overlapping dialogue, false starts and unfinished sentences, these films have all the hallmarks of fly-on-the-wall TV reportage. This, however, is quite misleading: they are, as Peter Lord puts it, 'almost a documentary but complete fiction!'

There has long been a difference of opinion between animators about what can and cannot be achieved in the medium. There are those who share the view expressed by Halas and Manvell in *The Technique of Film Animation*: 'In all animation, there should never be any doubt that what is being achieved on the screen could only be achieved by this means.' Others hold that any subject matter can be dealt with in animation and, indeed, the Disney studio's move towards making animated films of live-action stories, such as *Pocahontas* and *The Hunchback of Notre Dame*, suggests that audiences are not worried by the distinction. Kihachiro Kawamoto probably spoke for many in the animation business when he remarked: 'What interests me most in the production of animated film is that the person who creates it is the only one who can express what he feels, like a painter.'

That is certainly what Lord and Sproxton achieved in 'Animated Conversations' and 'Conversation Pieces'. Although the audio-track suggests that the characters on screen have been accurately drawn from life, the truth is more complex since the animation is, in fact, an imaginative interpretation of what is heard. By hearing the dialogue 'performed' by a realistic puppet - who may not bear any resemblance to the real owner of the voice - the words seems more sharply focused and the passing banalities of life take on a new significance.

The quiet desperation of the door-to-door salesman in the Lord and Sproxton film *Sales Pitch*, another in the 'Conversation Pieces' series.

For example, in *Sales Pitch*, an ever-hopeful door-to-door salesman gets into conversation with an elderly couple who are quite happy to chat, but who have clearly no intention of buying his mops and brushes. The desperation of the salesman - covered though it is by his easy, laughing manner - is painful to watch, and when he packs up his case and turns to go there is a moment where the audience glimpses the unnamed burdens that are weighing on his shoulders. At the same time, *Sales Pitch* is full of delightful comic character animation: the wife, saying little, deferring to the husband who abstractedly cleans out his pipe while the salesman relentlessly continues his pitch; the neighbour in an adjacent house, eavesdropping on the conversation, then accidentally banging her head on the open window; or the dog, seen at the end of the film chewing a sample brush.

One of the other films in this series was a significant departure. *Palmy Days* animated a rambling over-the-tea-cups conversation between several elderly people repeating oft-told tales and laughing politely at unfunny anecdotes. Peter Lord and Dave Sproxton could not, at first, see any value in this material, until they took a leap of the imagination, dressed the old folks in tattered clothes and palm-leaf skirts and placed them in a hut on a tropical island with a crashed plane in the background. By juxtaposing the surreal with the

A Burger King commercial, in which realistic-looking model versions of the product were combined with customers from the fantasy world of clay.

theatre, filmed in sombre colours and lit with harsh stage lighting that surrounds the actors with deep shadows.

In marked contrast to the theatricality of *Stage Fright* are Dave Riddett's and Luis Cook's *Knobs in Space* (1994), made for the Terrence Higgins Trust, and Sam Fell's *Pop* (1996), in which a quirky little character hopes to relieve his boredom with a can of fizzy drink which goes into orbit and finally blows his head off, leaving his vacated neck to be occupied by a singing goldfish.

As the company has grown, David Sproxton has increasingly taken on a supervisory role, overseeing much of the production work undertaken, particularly the commercials, though this means he has become less involved in a hands-on way with individual productions. The rapid growth of the company has also required it to assume a more formal structure, and a great deal of David's time is now spent in managing its affairs or, as he puts it, 'trying to make order out of chaos!'.

Meanwhile, Peter Lord continues directing his own films, such as *Wat's Pig* (1996), commissioned by Clare Kitson of Channel 4, who also took *Stage Fright*. This is a medieval fable - told with hardly any dialogue - about two brothers who are parted at birth. One brother becomes a king, the other a pig-keeper and their contrasting fortunes are shown in a unique split-screen format until a war with a neighbouring country unites their lives and their stories. *Wat's Pig* was nominated for an Academy Award, as was Lord's earlier film *Adam* (1991), in which a human (but also God-like) hand creates and then controls the existence of a little man whom Lord describes as being 'Morph with genitalia'. Having no dialogue, *Adam* works in the universal language of mime, and the film shows the subtlety of acting with clay which is Aardman's particular contribution to this form of animation.

Peter Lord is now embarked on the studio's latest venture, its first feature-length film. Jointly directed with Nick Park, the film - which is still in the early stages of development - is provisionally entitled *Chicken Run*, although, as with any film, that may change. All Peter Lord and Nick Park will reveal about the picture is that it could be described as *The Great Escape* - with chickens!

There is much public anticipation (and press speculation) about the project. There are those who think the studio should have stuck with the Oscar-winning formula of Wallace and Gromit. But that is not surprising. Over sixty years ago, when Walt Disney embarked on the cinema's first animated feature, *Snow White and the Seven Dwarfs*, there were those who shook their heads and said that he should stick to his Oscar-winning short cartoons featuring Mickey Mouse. Disney was undaunted and, as a result, animated feature films are now an accepted - and extraordinarily successful - part of today's film industry.

Nevertheless, whilst there have been hundreds of feature-length films made in cel animation, there have been relatively few three-dimensional animated features. However, the basic techniques remain the same, as does the sense of discovery - exciting, gratifying, but scary - that is unique to puppet animation.

'Rex the Runt', Richard Goleszowski's 13-part series, was launched on BBC Television in 1998.

'I always describe puppet animation,' says Peter Lord, 'as being instinctive. You go through it as you go through life: reasonably well-informed about what you've just done, with a plan for what you intend to do, but prepared also for an unpleasant surprise at any moment. You hold the puppet in your two hands, and maybe your left hand is holding the shoulders while your thumb lies commandingly on the spine. Your right hand is on the pelvis, ready to move either leg or both at once. So you've got the whole figure under your hand, ready to respond to your instruction. You can feel the movement in it, and the logic as it twists and bends. Often the puppet leads you, you can feel its inner life ...'

It is all very like those ancient creation myths in which some god or demi-god takes up a fistful of mud and shapes it into a thing that can hold, within its fragile form, all the passions, ambitions, dreams and despairs that are the lot of humankind - though without any certainty about how that creation will direct its own destiny.

basic needs

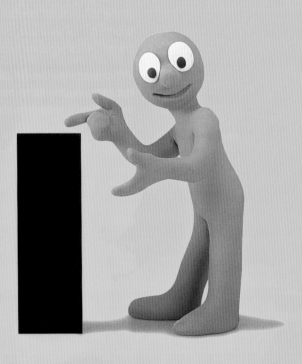

Video camera

★ **To calculate how far the camera should move during a pan or tilt, fix a pointer to the back of the camera head which follows an arc on a piece of cardboard. Basically, you divide the distance the camera has to move by the number of frames the move runs for. The move needs to accelerate to its full speed and then slow to a stop at the end. On the arc, mark off gradually increasing and decreasing increments for the first and last quarters of the move.**

35mm camera with connection for video assist (see pages 70-71) mounted on top of the camera body.

Video Cameras and Computer Animation

On the face of it, video has many advantages over cine film. These include low light exposure, auto exposure, reusable tape (making it cheaper to run), good picture quality, no need for a projector (you just watch it on TV), and instant replay. The big disadvantage is that the types of video camera available in the high street do not take single frames. Some boast an animation facility, but the best we know of take a quarter of a second per shot - the equivalent of 4.5 or 6fps on cine film. This is just not enough for smooth movement. You can certainly do some animation on a video camera, but the results will be crude compared with what you get using cine film.

Another approach would be to record your video images and store them on a computer. As computers become more popular, the ability to do this has become easier. We use a rather more sophisticated computer system at the studio to help the animators scrutinise their animation as they shoot it (see pages 70-71), but there are simpler and less expensive systems available which can run on home computers. These will play a few minutes of animation at a time. If longer lengths are needed, you would have to record the material in sections on to a video recorder. For the time being, however, most of these home computer systems do not match the quality of 8mm film, which remains the best system for learning about animation, as well as being much cheaper to run.

A further option is to buy software for video manipulation which can be used with a video or digital camera for stop-frame animation. For example, with Adobe Premiere's Stop-Motion feature you can make manual and time-lapse video captures. For stop-frame animation, you point the camera at your scene and record frames as you animate the sequence. You can then use the software to run your movie on the computer.

It is also possible to make animated films entirely on computers. At Aardman we have a small computer animation department that uses software called 'Softimage'. This very sophisticated package allows an animator to construct virtual puppets, clothe them, animate them and light them very much as we do for conventional filming. The technique is completely different but the animation skills needed are the same. Such systems are often used in special-effects movies, and entire films such as *Toy Story* have been created using these techniques. As ever with tools like these, you still have to have a good story to tell!

MOTION CONTROL

The most common camera moves are pans, where the camera scans sideways, and tilts, where it pivots up and down. You can also track a camera, moving the whole thing to one side, or forwards and backwards.

Any movement of the camera must be done smoothly, and there are various devices for controlling the camera as it moves. At the top end of the motion-control field is the Milo, right, a massive rail-mounted electrically driven computer-operated crane, with a boom arm that swivels on a revolving pedestal. This super-versatile rig allows the camera to be moved with optimum smoothness in just about any conceivable direction, its operation controlled by computer. It also repeats movements with extreme accuracy.

For Super 8 or 16mm cameras, buy a geared camera head which fits on top of the tripod. The head is equipped with handles which you turn to make a pan or tilt.

To track a camera sideways or on a curve, you only need some kind of wheeled support on to which you can fix the camera. For straight line movements, try a skateboard, guided along between planks. For greater variety you could use a wagon from a model train set, which you then push along a section of rail.

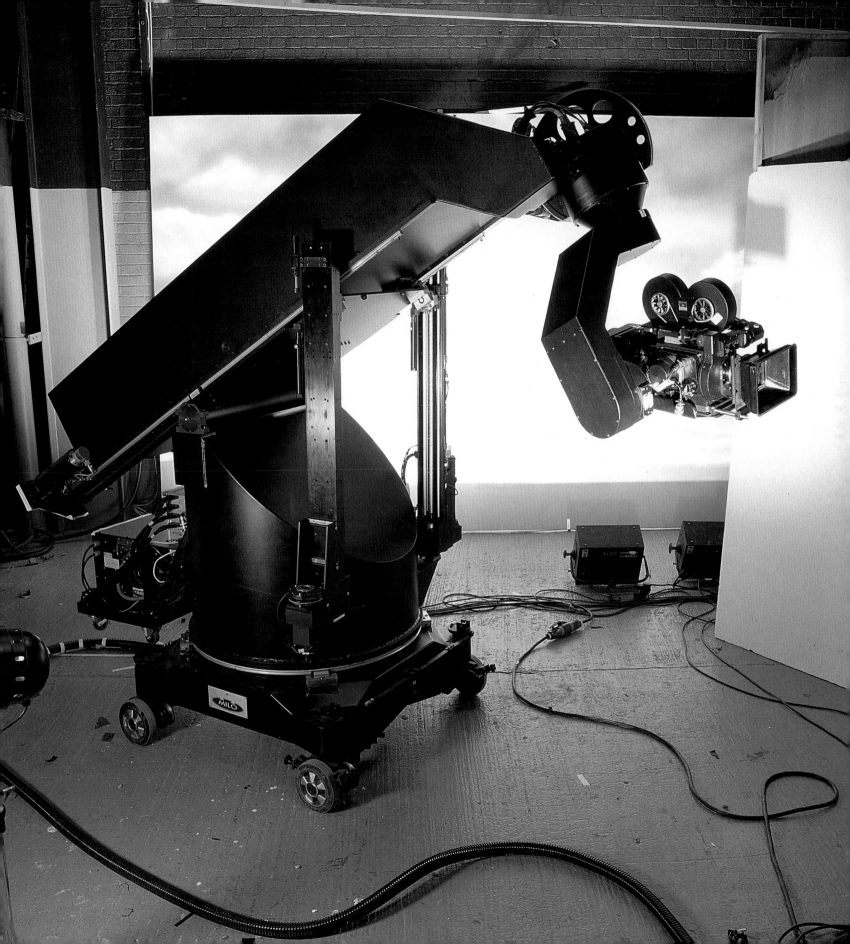

A Simple Studio

Our first studio was the kitchen in Dave's parents' house. Our stage was the kitchen table and our tripod was an old enlarging stand. In later years we moved up-market, first to the spare bedroom and later to his sister's room in the attic (which, I hasten to add, she had vacated). As this suggests, the basic requirements for a model-animation studio are very simple. You need your camera - film or video - and a computer (if that is your chosen method of storing the images). You need a tripod, to support the camera, a flat surface to act as a stage or set, and some lighting to ensure an unchanging level of light while you are animating. And, of course, your character, puppet or whatever.

There is one simple golden rule in the model-animation studio. Nothing should move unless you want it to. When most people start experimenting with animation - and that certainly includes us - the most common fault is that either the set, the shadows from the lights, the camera or the environment itself moves about almost as much as the animated puppet. Any part of your studio which is not firmly fixed down is liable to get knocked or jogged during the hours that you are animating, and every such movement becomes an irritating distraction in your finished film. To avoid this happening, everything possible needs to be fixed down, or otherwise rendered idiot-proof.

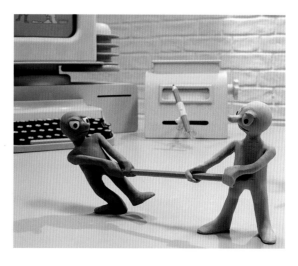

Of course, you have to be careful too. No camera, however sturdily fixed, is going to stay still if you clout it with the full force of your body. I notice that animators, even big clumsy ones, acquire in time great spatial awareness. They become instinctively aware of all the things they must not bump into and manage to avoid them - often without looking - with balletic elegance. Even so, we have to make sure that everything is fixed down.

You should be able to tighten your tripod so that the camera cannot slip, even over days. If, as we have already said, you can tape or otherwise fix the tripod legs to the floor, great. If not, try to weight it down so that a glancing blow will not shift it. Sometimes at Aardman we erect barriers - which could simply be ribbon or string - around the tripod, just to keep the animator at a safe distance from it.

Similarly, you do not want your table to start shifting. A succession of gentle nudges will appear like an earthquake in your finished film. The answer is to use

Morph and his mate Chas, deep in some squabble of huge unimportance. When Morph first appeared on BBC's 'Vision On', our brief was to provide a small blob-like character who would change into various shapes, charge around the table-top, and interact with presenter Tony Hart.

the most solid base you can. The table-top is your stage, and the surface should be appropriate. We will see later how models can be fixed to the table to hold their position, and some of these methods are fairly intrusive, involving pins or screws. It may be best not to use the actual table-top but to fix another surface to it. If you decide to do this, thick fibreboard is a good choice. If you follow the Aardman career path and start with clay models, you should be aware that oil and sometimes pigment can seep out of the clay and stain unvarnished wood. You may imagine that clay would stick well to a textured surface, but I found with Morph that he actually stuck best to something smooth and hard, like varnished wood, melamine or formica. If your chosen surface is a board laid on top of an existing table, make sure it is firmly clamped to the table.

A Complex Studio

As you can see, we have moved off the kitchen table. I love the studios at Aardman. I love the fact that they look, and sometimes feel, totally chaotic, though actually they are spaces which have evolved to be the way they are, and this includes being very efficient and businesslike. Even so, I hesitate to show them off to aspiring animators, in case they are discouraged by the complexity and technical sophistication.

In fact, however, the heart of a studio, no matter how complex it may seem, is the same as ever: model, set, camera and lights. We still use 35mm film cameras, though now we use them in conjunction with sophisticated devices that give us precise motion control (see page 66), allow us to plan a character's movements on-screen (video assist) and mix between one frame and the next one before shooting (digital frame store).

Video Assist When shooting on film, as we usually are, the only way to see the camera's view of a scene is by looking through the camera viewfinder. Video assist is a system for showing the same scene on a TV monitor. The big advantage is that it simplifies the real 3-D world into a two-dimensional world on the TV screen. To help ensure that your puppet is moving smoothly and evenly through the shot, you can draw on the screen with a water-soluble pen. If you trace, for example, the line of the character's back, you quickly find that after a few frames you have a pattern of lines on the screen that should be evenly spaced. Instead of guessing, or remembering how far your puppet has moved each frame, you can clearly see it on the screen. In our studios, a video camera is mounted to look through the film camera viewfinder, so that we can see *exactly* the view that will appear on film. You can approximate the same effect quite easily at home. Line up a video camera as close as possible to your film camera, and connect it to the TV. Clearly it helps if the video camera and film camera have the same lens angle so that the TV sees almost exactly what the film camera sees. At Aardman we go a step further. We use a computer-based video recorder which records each image on to disc. In this way we can play through the sequence of images already taken, and then add the one we plan to take next. After checking it to

The main characters in *Limoland* are singers Tina Turner, above, and Barry White, and because they appear in sets of different sizes we had to make them in two different versions. One set was the ordinary size for puppets, which is about 9in (23cm) high, and the other was double that.

This street set for *Limoland* is built on a steel table at the right height for animators to get in and out. We also left gaps for them between the buildings (which cannot be seen from the camera's viewpoint). To make things even more complex, we had to deal with a lot of 'practical' lights in the form of street lights, lights from cars and others in the buildings, all of which took a long time to set up.

see if it is OK, and adjusting the model if necessary, we record it on the computer, adding it to the end of the sequence, and then shoot the new image on the film camera. In fact, we are watching the animation develop frame by frame as we do it.

Digital Frame Store This looks rather like a small video mixing desk. We use it to store the image we have just taken, so that we can compare it with the one we are preparing to shoot. The frame store usually has a slider control so that the animator can mix gently between the two images, checking that every detail is correct. It is also invaluable for checking that nothing in the picture has moved that the animator did not want to move - or, in the case of the animator's worst disaster, when the puppet falls over during shot, it is possible to replace it in exactly the right position. We are now in the process of building the frame store into the video recorder so that everything is housed in one container.

The Power of Lighting

Today we use lighting in just the same way as a conventional film studio, except that we work on a much smaller scale with relatively tiny sets and characters. In order to achieve precise lighting control on such small sets, we use lanterns designed for use in theatres, called 'profile' lamps. These are designed a little like slide projectors and can project a very controlled beam from quite a distance. In this way lamps positioned some distance from the set can illuminate very small areas of it without 'spill light' falling on other areas.

The amount of light illuminating a set does not have to be huge as we use long shutter speeds, typically between one quarter to a full second exposure on moderately 'fast' film. It is possible to set a light quite adequately with a couple of anglepoise lamps. Some cameras have built-in light meters to help with exposure levels but, remember, the film is designed either for daylight use (which is a rather blue light) or tungsten (electric lamps) which gives a rather orange light. If the film type and light are mixed, a correction filter has to be used. This is usually placed over the camera lens. If a filter is used, exposure compensation needs to be made as the filter absorbs approximately one stop of light. Film lighting very often uses a three-source formula:

The **key light** gives the characters their shape, making distinctive and readable shadows. The lamp is often placed to one side of the camera and a little higher than the character to give a 'normal' look. One side of the face will be fully illuminated and the other will be in shadow, which will show the character's features well. If there is a window in the set, the key light will come from that direction to suggest that the light is coming through the window.

The **fill light** fills in the shadow side of the subject, keeping a reasonable difference between the two, typically one to two stops, to prevent the shadow side going totally black. To avoid multiple shadows, this light is often a 'soft' light, diffused by tracing paper or similar which is placed over the front of the lamp, or by 'bouncing' the light off a white card to produce a diffused source.

Lamps can be suspended from an overhead grid, right, or mounted, as below, on floor-mounted lighting stands.

The outer lamps in this group are fitted with Fresnel lenses which allow the beam angle to be adjusted.

Second and third from left are profile spots. Profile lamps give a more controllable beam of light which can be focused to give a hard-edged light or softened for a more subtle effect. Internal shutters can help to control the spread of light. You can also insert a 'gobo' - literally, something which comes between the lamp and the set. We use these to project a defined shape such as a window or a slatted venetian-blind pattern.

Over the front of the bigger lamps are 'barn doors' which help to control the spread of light and avoid unwanted spillage. Coloured gels can be either clipped to the barn doors (far left) or mounted in a frame that slots into the front of the lamp (third from right).

How lighting enhances the action. Clockwise from top left: Warm light from the fire is contrasted with the cold blue moonlight flooding in through the window; from *Wat's Pig*. *Film noir* suspense with deep shadows and a shaft of bright light in *The Wrong Trousers*. Car lights flash across the wall of the interview room in *Going Equipped*. Back lighting rims the worm/phallus shape of the character in *Ident* and makes him stand out from his background.

Bounced light is very useful, but the light 'falls off' (diminishes in power) very rapidly if the bounce board is too far from the subject.

The **back light** is used to 'rim' the subject with light, producing a highlight along all the top edges and separating the subject from the background. This is often called giving the subject 'an edge'. This light is placed quite high to the rear of the set pointing towards the camera. Care has to be taken not to have the light shining directly into the camera lens, so the lens may need to be shielded with a lens hood.

A very pleasing effect can be made using a 'three-quarter rear key'. This combines the effect of the back light and key light in one lamp by placing a lamp behind the subject and quite high, at about the 10 o'clock or 2 o'clock position. This gives strong shadows on the ground running towards the camera, and provides the subject with an edge as well as key-light modelling. The shadow side (facing the camera) is filled using soft light, and the exposure is made for the fill, with the result that the three-quarter key light looks bright and crisp.

73

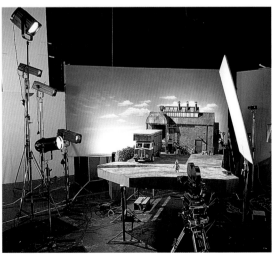

The lighting set-up for an outdoor shot in *A Close Shave*. For this shot the key light (1) assumes the sun position. The shadows are filled by 'bouncing' a narrow-beamed lamp (4) off the large white fill board (6). Three back lights (2,3,5) are used to give emphasis to certain parts of the set, such as the cabin of the truck and details on the rooftop. When positioning these, care is needed not to create secondary shadows from the camera's viewpoint (7).

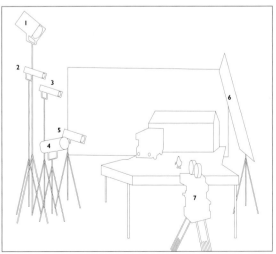

Preston at three times of day. For the daylight shot, left, the scene is keyed from the left as if the main source of light is from a high sun. The fill board to the right of the set bounces a soft light into the shadow areas.

Once your basic lights are in position, you can adjust the amount of light thrown on to the set by various means. First, think what kind of an overall effect you want. Do you want a bright, high-key look with little to no contrast - effectively shadowless - a style often used in comedies or to replicate an outdoor light without sun? Or do you want something more moody and low-key, with high contrast and plenty of shadows, the kind that goes best with thrillers?

Above left: It is dusk, and the scene is now keyed from the right using a lower light source and an added orange gel (filter) to give the impression of a setting sun. The advent of darkness is further emphasised by having very little frontal fill light and by using practicals such as the headlamps and lights in the building.

The direction of the key light is very important - it is the *key*. In everyday life, people are usually seen illuminated from above - from the sky - or from lights in the ceilings of buildings, so we read human faces with shadows falling down the face or across it, as from a low sun or as the light comes through a window. A light placed below the face makes it look abnormal and even horrific, especially if the light is coloured! Side lighting brings out the character in the face, emphasising the contours, and side frontal lighting softens the contours and produces a flattering look, as used in shots for glossy magazines.

Above: The cold quality of night-time is achieved by using a blue gel on the fill light contrasted with a warmer tungsten light source skimming over the building as if emanating from practical light sources.

Wiring up the headlight with a wire through the wheel arch. An important element in dressing and lighting night scenes is the use of 'practicals' such as these headlamps (actually torch or flashlight bulbs) which are connected to a low-voltage power supply.

Soft back light can be produced by placing the lamp beside the camera and directing its beam over the top of the set to bounce off a white or foil-covered board above and behind the set. This gives good rim-lighting effects, but the lamp will need to be quite a bit stronger than the key light to read adequately.

Another good effect is to throw shadows on the wall of a set to look like sunlight pouring in through a window. Cut a window-frame shape out of card and place this close to the set and some distance away from a spotlight, positioning it so that it produces a slanting 'sun beam' across the wall. Putting a light orange filter on the light source will make it even more convincing.

simple techniques

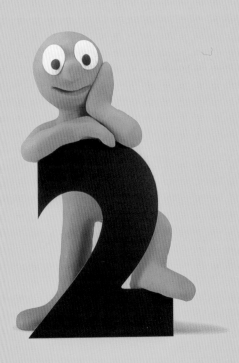

Simple Clay Animation

Working with modelling clay (Plasticine) is the perfect way to get started in animation. As a material it is cheap, flexible and instantly ready to use. Within minutes of opening the pack, you can be animating (not necessarily well, it is true, but certainly animating). So where to start? You have a camera, an empty table and a pack of clay. Take a piece of clay and roll it round in your hands to warm it up. Now practise some moves with it - let it stand up and flip over. Divide it into two lumps. Make them rotate around each other. Each time you move one forward, say 0.5in (1.2cm), press down on it a little. As it moves, it flattens itself. Let one piece grow taller. Before you move it, mark its position on the table with a loop of clay, lift it off the set, squeeze it out longer, then put it back on its mark. Look through the camera and check the new position.

Top: A simple bar of clay, straight from the pack - and never mind the finger-prints! Make it stand up, flip over and break into fragments.

Left: The raw material of clay animation. For filming we use English clay, firmer than the American type which is softer and has brighter colours. Clay is a simple tool, and you need no training to get started. There is nothing to stand between you - the creator - and your ideas.

Try to relax and not be too ambitious at first. Although you could go directly to making a clay figure, a little person or animal, that would be to risk becoming bogged down too soon in detail. Even at this first stage in animation, there are rules and techniques which are simple to follow and will enormously improve the finished result. Never forget that the frame you are animating is one of a sequence. It is not an end in itself. Never lose sight of how slow animation is. If you are working in double-frame, 12 separate moves will only make one second of animation. Time yourself going through a movement to get a sense of how fast your puppet can or should move. How much can you do, how far can you move in one second? If you have a stop-watch, use this to time movements. If not, try saying 'Tick-tock' at a normal rate of speaking; this takes about one second. If you need one second to move, say, 5 ft (1.5m), this means you can film your puppet travelling an equivalent distance - perhaps a complete walk cycle - in 12 frames. Divide up this space into 12 sections or frames to pinpoint each move.

Above: From a blob to a Morph in five moves. This is not so easy, and it would be wise to practise first with the simple sequences on this and the following pages. Have fun with what clay does so well. It is organic and flexible. Each sequence gives you 8-10 phases of movement, or nearly 1 second of film in double-frame (12fps). Put in 3-4 still frames at the beginning to announce your film, and 3-4 at the end to close it.

Opposite: Room set ready for the opening shot. Objects such as the jug and glasses, and the base of the anglepoise, will remain in a fixed position throughout. Plan your own film with this in mind, allowing later arrivals enough space to perform their moves. At the beginning of your film, shoot 2-3 seconds of the same frame to establish the scene before everything starts moving, and to freeze it at the end when the action comes to a climactic halt.

Simple Object Animation

Most of this book is concerned with animating models in miniature sets. It is also perfectly possible to animate in the real world, using full-sized objects as props and employing the human body - your own or someone else's - as the puppet. When real people and locations are used, the process is called 'pixillation', the word suggesting the idea of figures jumping about as though bewitched. Because you do not have to build either sets or models, it is a wonderful medium for fast, improvised animation.

These techniques are not part of our mainstream work, but most of us at Aardman have experimented with pixillation early on in our careers, and most of us will jump at the opportunity to do it because it is great fun. While conventional animation requires the animator to work quietly and intensively on his or her own, pixillation is a process in which several people can animate, or be animated, at the same time.

There are masses of things you could animate in a room. They include: an anglepoise lamp; a clothes airer; a glass that fills and empties with liquid; a chest of drawers opening and shutting; curtains and blinds which open and close; a cupboard which opens and the contents jump out; books which change places; toys; things with wheels; counterweighted light fittings, and anything made in several sizes of the same design - weights from scales, saucepans, plates, Russian dolls.

When you lay out your set for object animation, think first of the end point and how to work towards it. Not everything has to be in the opening sequence. Bring some objects in later to create a surprise. Examples from our shots overleaf are: the abacus next to the guitar, the clothes airer, and the dominoes and Lego pieces which jump out of the box. Try to create relationships between the pieces: the clothes airer does not just yaw up and down, it also moves sideways towards the chest, the drawers of which open to allow towels and a scarf to slither out and on to the airer's rails. You need only a minimum of aids to make a room scene work: use tacky putty to hold the rug in position, and suspend the towels and scarf with cotton. As ever, when you move something to animate it, like the jug or glasses, be sure to mark its position with a loop of clay or tacky putty *before* you lift it. When selecting your camera position, choose a viewpoint where everything can be seen clearly and without distortion; in our example the lens is approximately at the eye-level of someone standing.

Above: Frames from our Channel 4 Television logo sequence, made by animating the chest of drawers and the number 4, which squeezes in and out of various drawers. The beach location is an extra bit of surreal fun which makes the chest look more interesting than it would in a room setting.

Now the action starts. On the left, the baseball cap creeps up the wall unit, the cupboard door opens, a poster starts to unravel and the first tennis racquet comes into view. The clothes airer jumps across the room, in the corner there is now an abacus next to the guitar, and more and more cushions arrive on the sofa. In the foreground, the lamp comes on and focuses with rising astonishment on the box and its contents. The dominoes dance off in one direction and the Lego pieces turn themselves into tower blocks. Meanwhile, the glasses fill with orange juice and the jug empties. In the background, the curtains part, the blind slides up and flowers multiply like rabbits.

See how many other animated objects you can find in the pictures. If you make your own film, think about the story behind it all. Perhaps this is what happens every day, when the humans are out of the house and the things come out to play. Run the film backwards, and everything goes back to normal.

Dancing spoons, arranged in a serpentine layout, as made for the Golden Syrup commercial. A metal spoon, being inflexible, is typical of the objects we animate by substitution, shooting a separate model, or group of models, for each frame of film.

Other Animation Techniques

There is a very particular technique of puppet animation called 'substitution' that I always associate with the Dutch animator George Pal. Although I am sure he did not invent the technique, he raised it to a fine art. Substitution is utterly different from other forms of puppet animation, and actually has more in common with drawn animation. Instead of having one puppet which is repositioned, you use a separate model for each frame of film. Shooting in double-frame, you would need 12 separate models for 1 second of film. We have used the technique only a few times, for TV commercials, and although it is absurdly labour-intensive in the modelmaking department, and expensive, the results can be very satisfying.

Substitution has three main advantages. Firstly, it offers a way of articulating materials that are otherwise very difficult to animate because for some reason they will not bend. For example, a character made out of shiny metal or glass is impossible to animate conventionally (the normal solution today would be to create a computer-generated character). However, you can make a series of models with a chrome finish and shoot them individually.

Secondly, the technique allows the sort of graphic exaggeration that is common in 2-D animation. George Pal used this to great effect in his films. A puppet's walk cycle can include extravagant stretching of the limbs, as demonstrated by the marching figures in the illustrations. With this kind of animation a puppet can change its mass from one frame to the next. Finally, if an action is repeated, it can be quite efficient to build an animation cycle. This is what we did for the Golden Syrup commercial, where all the puppets were required to do was to walk in a repeating cycle.

Substitution need not be the complicated and expensive process that I have outlined. You can make simple and very effective substitution cycles out of clay. This could be as simple as a bouncing-ball sequence, where the clay model shows all the squash and stretch usually associated with 2-D animation. To be a little more complicated, you could make a series of walking figures to show the legs reaching out in an exaggerated way. When you work with this technique, you can emphasise the importance of bodyweight in motion, letting the character almost sag into the ground and spring upward with each step, like a human bouncing ball.

Marching figures animated by substitution, also for the Golden Syrup commercial. The bread is from a giant loaf baked specially for us. The baker cut it in slices and we put these in plywood formers to go stale, so the slices would stay in the required shape during filming.

87

models and modelmaking

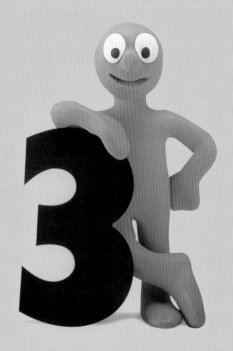

Basic Principles

You have got your storyboard, at least in outline, and perhaps a few sketches of the character you want to make. Now is the time to think in some detail about the nature of the model and what you want it to do. Think about its size, shape, weight, and the kind of movements you need it to perform.

How big should you build it? If it is too small, there will not be room to accommodate the mechanical skeleton, known as an armature, which allows the model to be posed and to hold its position. The advantage of a larger model is that you can give it plenty of detail. On the other hand, the larger the model the larger the set has to be, and that can present its own problems. For many of our films we make the human-shaped characters about 8-10in (20-25cm) tall, and construct everything else to fit round this scale.

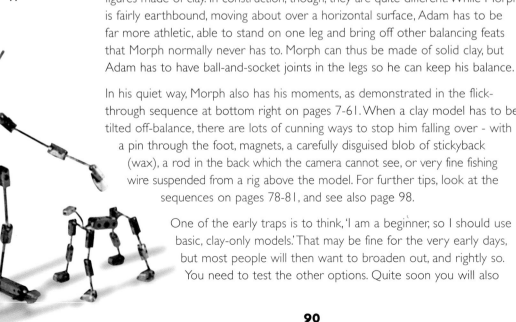

Morph has always been hand-made. To check that we always used the same amount of clay, we weighed him on these old scales.

Armatures for Wallace and Gromit. These mechanical skeletons are precisely designed and built from detailed drawings of the character (see page 99). You can make them yourself, though most amateur animators get theirs from specialist suppliers.

Weight, too, can be a problem. Say you have a character with a big head. Even if you use a hollow head, it will still need special support. How much support? Will a simple wire skeleton be enough, or will it need a tougher rod-and-joint armature? As ever, it is a balancing act between the artistic requirements of how big the head must be, and the practical question of how you can make that shape work.

Outwardly, Morph and Adam may look very similar. Both are human-shaped figures made of clay. In construction, though, they are quite different. While Morph is fairly earthbound, moving about over a horizontal surface, Adam has to be far more athletic, able to stand on one leg and bring off other balancing feats that Morph normally never has to. Morph can thus be made of solid clay, but Adam has to have ball-and-socket joints in the legs so he can keep his balance.

In his quiet way, Morph also has his moments, as demonstrated in the flick-through sequence at bottom right on pages 7-61. When a clay model has to be tilted off-balance, there are lots of cunning ways to stop him falling over - with a pin through the foot, magnets, a carefully disguised blob of stickyback (wax), a rod in the back which the camera cannot see, or very fine fishing wire suspended from a rig above the model. For further tips, look at the sequences on pages 78-81, and see also page 98.

One of the early traps is to think, 'I am a beginner, so I should use basic, clay-only models.' That may be fine for the very early days, but most people will then want to broaden out, and rightly so. You need to test the other options. Quite soon you will also

Building a wire-based figure - one of the troupe of chihuahuas featured in *Stage Fright*. Wire figures are easier to animate than clay models, and cheaper to make than armatured characters, but tend to snap if too much is demanded of them.

discover that unsupported clay is not all that easy to animate. It smudges and gets dirty, and you have to clean it and resculpt every two or three shots. Because of its weight, it is also relatively inflexible.

You might do better to go for a wire-based figure which has its rigid parts, such as the head, made of balsa wood or fibreglass to cut down on weight, and its skeleton covered with foam or cloth. A figure made like this will last longer and let you do more with it. It will also, by keeping its shape, retain the essentials of the character. This is important. With clay, you can shave off so many bits between shots, or unintentionally pull it so far out of shape, that you end up with a different-looking character. This will not endear you to audiences, who need to identify with a character that remains consistent and recognisable.

Don't be afraid to experiment. The more you do, the more you will build up an armoury of different solutions which you can apply in different contexts. At Aardman, in the course of designing and building a single character, we will look at dozens of different materials. In modelmaking there is no neat set of perfect answers. Every character calls for a different way of working.

Sometimes you do not need to build a whole character for a particular sequence. For a head-and-shoulders shot, it can be enough to build the top half of the body and put it on a central pole. As long as the character is held stable for the shot, it does not need to have legs as well.

Think also about the character's focus of interest. If a character has expressive hands, these will probably need a special armature. In *Loves Me ... Loves Me Not*, the character has to have long-fingered, extra-flexible hands so he can perform the delicate task of plucking individual petals off a flower. Hands break easily, by the way, so with a character like that you will need to make several replacement hands which can then be pegged on to the arm as required. To do this, you need to allow for a hole at the end of the arm when you design the basic figure.

As you can see, there is a lot of planning involved. It is a bit like cooking, really. You have to put in all the ingredients to get the right result. And in modelmaking, of course, you have to write the recipe as well.

The compulsive petal-plucking hero of *Loves Me ... Loves Me Not*. Because of the delicacy of his hand movements, and the amount of times he repeats the action, special armatures were made for his hands.

Wallace makes vain shooing noises at the horde of sheep happily camped out in his living room. Even though these sheep may seem to be mere extras, the detailing on them is precise. Necks and heads move about, and the eyes are surmounted by vast lids made of fast-cast resin.

Making a Sheep

In modelmaking terms, there are three types of sheep in *A Close Shave*, which we broadly categorised as Normal Sheep, Stunt Sheep and Thin Sheep. Thin Sheep were required for the scene in the wool shop when they run between Wallace and Wendolene, and we needed to show a mass of different woolly shapes going past while Wallace and Wendolene are still holding hands over their heads. They, obviously, had much narrower bodies than the normal type. Stunt Sheep were used for the shot where they plunge through the small trapdoor in Wallace's house, and when Shaun emerges shivering from the Knit-O-Matic. They had to be different again, with a lighter and more squashy build, and had skeletons made of mesh and coiled wire. Normal sheep were really quite complex, and had a variety of options built into their basic armature. This was made of K&S square-section metal tubing, and had two sets of holes in

Right: Sketch of Shaun the Sheep as he swings to the rescue on board the anvil. Drawings such as this help the animator to see the shot in advance, and also give the modelmaker clues about how the model should be constructed.

each corner so that the sheep's legs could either come out vertically (for the normal standing position) or out at the sides for the pyramid scene when the sheep are on Wallace's motorbike. Again, there were special holes to allow the neck to fit into the body at different points, depending on the shot. When the sheep form a tower outside the prison (while Shaun saws through the bars and rescues Gromit), their heads are naturally forced downwards by the weight of the sheep on top, and so their necks had to be set lower on the body. In the usual standing position, the head was set higher up on the body.

On the following pages we show the various construction stages for a Normal Sheep. These involve a bewildering array of materials which we have learned about through experience (also known as trial and error), ranging from the K&S armature down to tiny details like the glass-bead eyes with painted pupils.

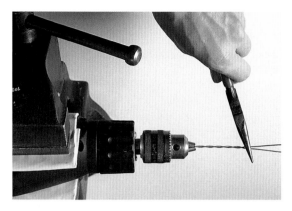

Left-hand column: Legs are made from lengths of twisted aluminium wire.

The feet are steel discs with holes for the leg and for a pin in case the leg needs extra support.

The leg is covered in mesh which is cut to size and squeezed round the aluminium wire.

The head is made of fast-cast resin. Once out of the mould, the holes and slots for eyes and ears are drilled to shape with an electric drill.

Right-hand column: The first stage completed, with pieces of K&S square-section tubing added last to join the legs to the body.

The eyes are white glass beads with pupils painted on using a paint brush and enamel paint. First, the glass bead is placed on a cocktail stick, then put in a drill and clamped with a vice. The drill is turned on to run slowly while the pupil is painted.

A covering of Plastazote - a hard, foam-like material - is put over the metal armature and trimmed with a scalpel, leaving the various holes clear for fitting the legs, neck and tail.

The ears are made of aluminium wire which is twisted to leave a loop at one end. Over the loop goes a piece of mesh, and over this goes the outer covering of maxi-plast rubber, which is sculpted and baked in an oven to retain its shape.

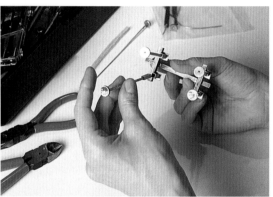

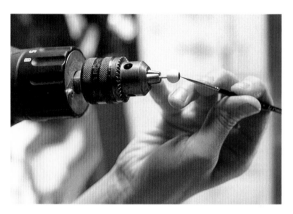

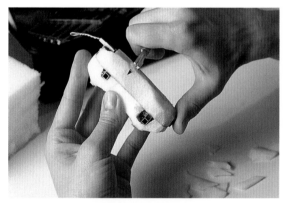

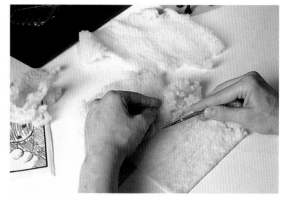

Left-hand column: The second stage completed, with **Plastazote** body and legs made of maxi-plast rubber which has been sculpted and baked.

Next, the body and tail are covered with a square of foam, which is trimmed to shape with scissors.

Right-hand column: Fur fabric, the final covering, is starched to make it lie down properly and avoid flickering on film. It is then trimmed from its backing, top, and glued over the foam layer, as shown in the next picture.

Eyelids are cast in coloured resin and then trimmed to shape. When the head is finally assembled, the ears and neck are glued into the head with epoxy-resin glue. The eyes, however, are bedded into a type of sticky wax which holds them in place but allows movement.

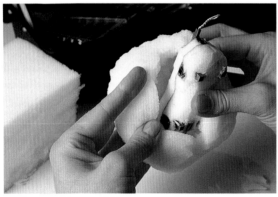

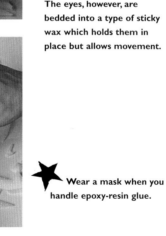

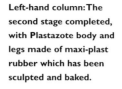 Wear a mask when you handle epoxy-resin glue.

Wat Construction

Wat and his brother, in *Wat's Pig*, are good examples of the human-type everyman figure. When planning the model, we knew that he would have to move fluidly and often, and make a lot of emphatic gestures. The solution was to keep his build fairly spindly, as the drawing opposite shows. Basically, the head consists of a solid core covered with clay and sculpted, and the hands are also made of clay. The rest of the body is made of foam applied sparingly over a metal armature.

Construction falls into several main stages. It begins with the storyboard, where the film-maker can give real purpose to any previous sketches he may have made of the character. Once the story is working properly, the character's design can be finalised and drawn up. The figure is then sculpted in clay and a design drawing made for the armature. This shows in detail how the armature will be built and how it fits inside the character. When the armature is made, it is wrapped in plumber's tape to make a better bond with the latex covering. The clay sculpture is broken down into its component parts, such as the torso, and these are cast in plaster. This produces a plaster mould in which the armature is placed and coated with foam latex. The mould is baked and the finished torso (or whatever) is removed ready for colouring and assembly with the head, legs and hands.

Wat and his brother, shown in split screen, essentially two characters cast from the same mould.

Making the armature is a delicate and specialist task, nothing less than engineering in miniature. This picture shows the modelmaker surrounded by the tools of his trade: in the foreground, vernier calipers, allen keys, assorted pliers and a hacksaw.

A mobile model such as this needs good built-in stability to help it stand up when its weight is not in the vertical plane. There are various ways to achieve this, the best being to fit a three-part footplate to the armature, as shown in the skeleton on the right. These footplates spread the weight of the model over a broad area and allow the animator to move the foot in a convincing way when the model itself is in motion. Other solutions to the stability problem are to hammer a pin into the foot and hide it with a blob of clay, suitably coloured. Alternatively, use a stickyback, a small blob of wax, which you can mix with clay to disguise it, and then apply it to stick down the foot at the appropriate point. Another option is to use a pair of magnets: one is fixed in the foot and the other is placed on the underside of the stage. If these solutions are not enough, as when the model is standing on one leg or leaning or holding something, you can put a piece of stout wire in its back to act as a prop, and then anchor this in a blob of clay behind the figure, where it will be out of sight of the camera. To make your model tilt over, or fall or fly, put fine fishing wire around the waist and neck and hang the figure from a rig positioned out of shot. Against a white background the wire will probably be invisible. If not, hide it by spraying it in a colour that matches the background.

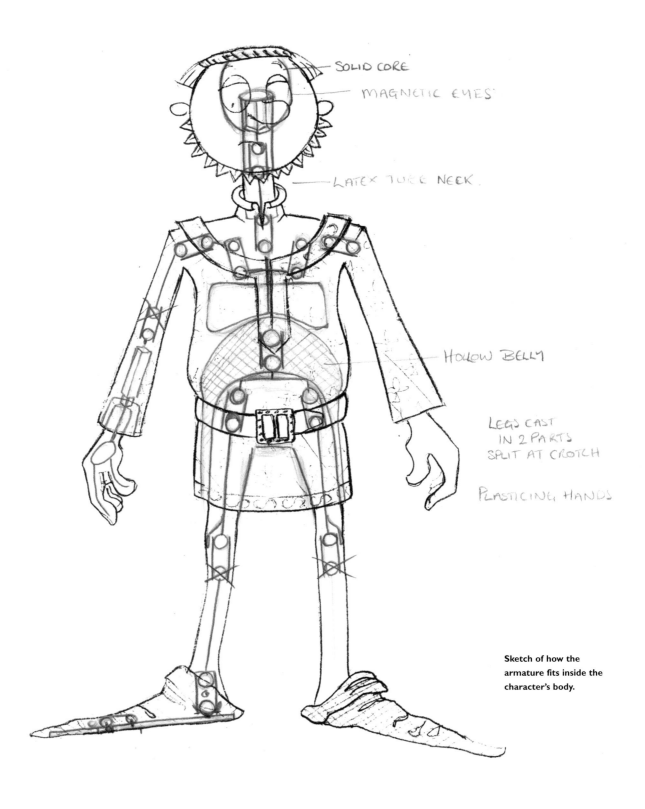

SOLID CORE

MAGNETIC EYES

LATEX TUBE NECK.

HOLLOW BELLY

LEGS CAST
IN 2 PARTS
SPLIT AT CROTCH

PLASTICINE HANDS

**Sketch of how the
armature fits inside the
character's body.**

The original Wat figure is
sculpted in Plasticine
(modelling clay) on a simple
wire armature. This has brass
square-section fittings so
that all the component parts
can easily be taken apart.

The clay torso is laid up,
ready to be cast in plaster.

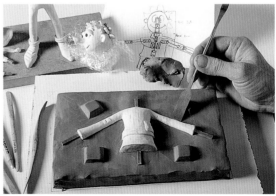

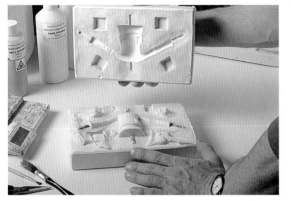

Left-hand column: Foam latex is brushed into the plaster mould, with the ball-and-socket armature wrapped in tape. The mould is separated after baking, the foam latex torso is removed and any excess foam is trimmed off.

Right-hand column: Colouring the torso with a diluted latex mixture. To colour figures, you can either spray the whole torso with the main colour and then hand-paint details such as the belt, or you can mask out the parts you do not want covered and spray the rest.

Assembling the puppet after painting.

Sculpting the hands in clay. A character such as Wat will use a lot of hand gestures in the course of a film, which means the hands will need replacing from time to time with new ones.

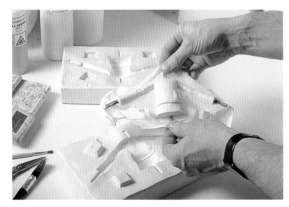

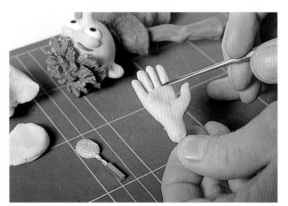

Rex Construction

Rex the Runt and the main characters in his series of adventures are flattish, not unlike gingerbread men. Their shape, and the way they are made, comes from the special way the series is filmed. This is the so-called 2-D technique of shooting the characters on an angled sheet of glass, often with a painted or photographic background positioned behind the glass so that the two elements can be combined in a single shot. Rex and the others - Wendy, Bad Bob and Vince - are not completely two-dimensional (even a gingerbread man has a certain minimal depth) but the way they can be used is very different from a fully rounded, three-dimensional character.

There are three main advantages to shooting on glass. Firstly, you do not need the complex armatures which have to be built for most of our conventional 3-D characters, such as Wallace and Gromit. Secondly, the characters are not bound by gravity and can be animated to jump or fly around the scene, more like they do in cel animation. Thirdly, the animator can sit in reasonable comfort at the sheet of glass, which is fixed at the angle of a drawing-board, with the camera shooting over the animator's shoulder.

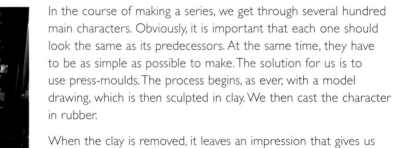

Rex and Vince, ready for the camera. Once the basic figure is sprung from the press mould, the eyes, noses and clothing are added. The eyes consist of simple white beads with small holes in the pupil so the eye can be moved around expressively. Noses are made of solid resin, and Rex's mouth is a loop of clay.

In the course of making a series, we get through several hundred main characters. Obviously, it is important that each one should look the same as its predecessors. At the same time, they have to be as simple as possible to make. The solution for us is to use press-moulds. The process begins, as ever, with a model drawing, which is then sculpted in clay. We then cast the character in rubber.

Animating on glass. The characters are set up on the angled glass, often with a suitable background placed behind it, then filmed from a position over the animator's shoulder.

When the clay is removed, it leaves an impression that gives us the press mould. This is then surrounded by a plaster jacket to stop the mould distorting. The mould can be reused throughout the production to turn out new characters when they are needed.

Once the mould is ready for use, the first step is to dust it with talcum powder to prevent the clay from sticking to it. Then a thin layer of clay is rolled out and pressed into the mould. This is followed by more clay, pushed in carefully to make sure it works its way into all the detailing of the figure. The top surface is finally flattened out with a rolling pin. To extract the completed character from the mould, the trick is to bend it slowly and at just the right angle for it to pop out. The character is then ready for the usual finishing work - adding the eyes, nose, mouth and any other special features, such as Bad Bob's eye patch.

Above: A complete impression of the figure lies in the rubber mould after casting, while the modelmaker rolls out a thin layer of clay.

Centre left: Layers of clay are pressed into the mould and pushed into all the details of the figure.

Centre right: When the mould is full, it is flattened with a rolling pin.

Below: The rubber mould is separated from its plaster jacket and then gently bent to release the new figure.

Preston

Preston is the evil dog in *A Close Shave* who first appears as the thuggish sheep-rustler who rules the roost in Wendolene's blighted household. At the film's climax, he is transformed into a metallic monster, receives his just desserts and ends up as a crippled robotic wreck. He is thus seen in three completely different versions - the brutal but recognisably doggy dog, the gleaming robo-dog and the trembling has-been.

John Wright, who specialises in 'engineered' models, made the original armature for the basic Preston, which was then modelled in clay and dressed with the character's special spiked collar and wrist bands. The other, mechanical versions are much more elaborate and were made in John Wright's workshop in Bristol. He recalls, 'What was interesting about the robot Preston was that his armature was on the outside and became part of his villainous character.'

The arms and legs are in fact part of a basic armature, with the visible parts dressed with extra screws and piping to make them look more mechanical and threatening. The body was machined in a chemical-wood material called Modelling Board and painted with a steel-finish paint. This was then dirtied up around the rivets to make it look as if it had been knocked about.

On the chest (see main picture, right) is a miniature tape recorder, also specially made. The other main feature of this model is a hinge at the back of the head which allows the top of the head to lift back and reveal a mouth horrifically full of cogs, gears and piping.

Finally, after his disastrous experience in the Mutton-O-Matic, the crippled Preston is a mere shadow of his former brute self. The body is essentially the same, though tipped over into the horizontal, but in place of his fierce armature-legs he now stands on four much more spindly supports, made to look like wall units for a shelving system and mounted on pram wheels. For added pathos he sports a bandage wrapped round his forehead.

The three ages of Preston, in which the villainous bully dog is transformed into a metal robot clad in spikes, pipes and rivets, and later, after meeting a machine which is even bigger than he is, emerges a beaten-up, bandaged wreck gliding about on pram wheels.

set design and making

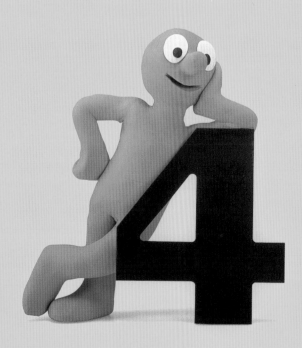

The Jaguar mourns the lack of space in his simple brick enclosure; from *Creature Comforts*.

Planning a Set

For about the first ten years of our career, Dave and I never had a set with more than three walls in it. That really is all you need at first, just something that neatly contains the miniature world you are filming.

Every set has to have a firm base which does not move. Even though your basic stage or tabletop may be solid and flat, it is a good idea to build each set with its own floor. It will then be completely transportable and can be stored out of the way when you do not need it, and brought back for use in another film. Also, your basic stage will soon get mucky and stop being very flat if it has to be host to a succession of different sets. Use a sheet of hardboard or plywood as the platform and colour it with emulsion paint.

As you design your set, think about where you will want to bring in the camera. In relative scale, the camera is about as big as a double-decker bus, so you have to make plenty of allowance for it. Think, too, about how you will light your set and leave enough space to get in and animate your characters, whether from the front, the side or by moving in over the top. Try to avoid situations where you risk brushing against, and moving, any part of the set. This is easier said than done, but if you move something and do not put it back exactly where it was, the shift will show up on your film.

Try to keep your first sets indoors, and confine everything within a space of about 4ft × 4ft (1.2m × 1.2m). For a simple room set, build two side walls and a back wall from foamboard or thick card. Cut out a window in a side or rear wall to give yourself extra lighting and shadow options. Hold the walls upright with supports glued on to the back, and fix the walls to the floor with blobs of tacky putty. If you need to take out a wall to shoot from a different angle, be sure to mark its position before you lift it.

The furniture and other props need not be elaborate. Add simple chairs and a table if this fits the plot of your story. Look around local toy and model shops for ready-made pieces, or make everything yourself from simple materials such as balsa wood. Glue the parts together and colour them. Later you can move on to scenic artist's paints, but for now any water-based paint will do. If you want a tree to be visible outside the window, make the trunk and branches from a frame of twisted aluminium wire, cover it with masking tape and paint it. Cut leaves from coloured paper and glue them on to small frames of fine mesh, of the kind used to patch holes in the bodywork of cars.

Wallace in his sitting room, basically a simple three-walled set with a window on one side, through which different lighting effects could be used to suggest changes in the weather or time of day.

Bear in mind that props should be more or less in scale with your characters, and that most human-shaped puppets are 8-10in (20-25cm) tall. Remember, too, that nothing has to be spot-on realistic. You are operating in a world populated by small clay creatures, and the important thing is that their chairs, their TV sets, cars and other worldly goods should look appropriate to them.

A Straightforward Set

From an entry-level set with just three walls, it is not such a big jump to Wallace and Gromit's sitting-room. The basic structure is the same, even though it is made with greater expertise and has more elaborate furniture and décor.

Our conventional room sets are free-standing table units. The whole structure has to be strong and solid enough not to move under temperature and atmospheric changes. The floors are usually made of perforated steel, which is strong enough not to bend and thin enough for magnets positioned underneath to hold and draw the puppets as they move around the set. The actual room finish - in the form of floorboards, carpet and so on - is fixed over the floor. The room walls are usually made of plywood and fixed in position by means of dowels - like pack-flat furniture - so they can be lifted out easily when shots need to be taken through the space they are occupying.

You can apply the same techniques to other more complicated sets such as a staircase and landing. Here, it is important to leave sufficient space under the stairs for the animators to get in and reposition the magnets - and to do so many times during the course of a sequence.

Outdoor and Landscape Sets

Outdoor sets are generally bigger and more difficult because you have different layers from front to back, and this all takes up a lot more space than a room set. In *Wat's Pig*, for

Set drawing for *Wat's Pig*, with Wat outside his hovel and the ground sloping up and away towards the castle. Opposite, a frame from the film shows the same scene.

Below is the same landscape seen from side-on. From the platform on the far right, where the characters stand, the ground rolls away in layers towards the horizon and painted sky.

example, we had a landscape set with three layers, and a trck running through it. First was the foreground which sloped upwards from a flat plain that the characters could stand on. This was about 8ft (2.4m) deep. Then the land appeared to fall away - in fact it was a gap with nothing at all there - and behind that we had the next layer of hills, which was about 2ft (60cm) from front to back. However, the track appeared much narrower so the audience would understand that it was much farther away. Behind this was the third layer of hills with the castle perched on top.

These hills were painted in paler colours to make them recede, and in the far background was a painted sky. It was all very graphic rather than realistic, but it suited the context of a fabled medieval world inhabited by peasants, warriors, a power-mad baron and a kindly smiling pig.

Matching Sets to Products

When the function of a set is to help advertise a product, it will tend to look more highly finished than usual. This is particularly true of scenes where the product itself is presented in some form. Clients want their product to look good, and sometimes the tone of a commercial is worked out from that point.

This by no means applies to all commercials, many of which take place in a complete fantasy land which is geared to promoting some idea about the product or special quality that the advertising agency has chosen to emphasise - its great taste, for example, or the fact that it is made of real fruit. However, when the product appears in the story, it will probably be handled straight, pretty much as you would see it in real life or in a brochure. In our commercials for Burger King, we peopled the set with a colourful mob of clay puppets, but the burgers, buns, chips, etc were handled in a realistic manner.

To make such items is specialist work, and here the boundaries become blurred between modelmaking and set-building. Whoever does the work, the important thing is to get the right blend between the animated models and the backgrounds against which they move. This can be seen in the Polo commercials, where the sturdy shape of the mints, with their chunky embossed lettering, seems to express a sympathetic bond with the shiny metal machines in the Factory of the Future (courtesy of 1930s Hollywood) which is obviously dedicated to production of the ultimate mint, and where every surface is studded with Polo-like rivets.

In our Chevron commercials, we were dealing with a product which is virtually impossible to show - petrol. To resolve this, we created a range of vehicles which run on Chevron (and others that do not) and made them into central figures. They are strong characters with expressive features: the headlights are eyes, which swivel this way and that, their radiator grilles are mouths and their wipers act as highly mobile eyebrows. The sets were then matched to the cars, right down to the last

High-finish factory sets for the Polo commercials, crammed with glass and metal surfaces held together by Polo-shaped rivets.

Wide-eyed and expressive, with wiper eyebrows and radiator mouths: two cars from the Chevron series.

Drawing for a Polo factory set, which by featuring an impressive length of conveyor belt, moving in a bold diagonal across the set and surrounded by machines, goes far beyond the conventional three-walled space of most 3-D animation sets.

petrol pump and telegraph pole, so that everything had the same graphic 'cartoon' quality. In other words, we built a believable world for those characters to inhabit.

Many advertisements finish by cutting to a pack shot of the product. You may see the company name and logo as well as the product, or just the product by itself. For this we often make a special larger version, it being much easier to make something look good if you make it bigger than life-size and build up its inherent textures. These packs may even be more perfect than the ones on sale in the supermarket. We can do this by taking off the bar code, for example, or some tiny detail such as a copyright line.

Then the pack has to sit perfectly in its setting, on a velvet cushion or surrounded by petals, each of which has to be exquisite and just right. All this adds a sense of high quality, hence desirability, which the client naturally wants people to associate with this particular product.

113

A Complex Set

The film *Stage Fright* started off as the story of an entertainer who passed through all the showbiz eras of this century. Beginning as a dog-juggler in music hall, he went into silent movies, then he tried talkies, and so on, and each time he failed in some dreadful way to make a go of it. As the planning went on, we could see it would be possible to make almost the entire film in a single music-hall setting, and this encouraged us to invest heavily in building one big set.

The theatre is based on the Bristol Old Vic, and we show it in two periods. One belongs to the cheerful past, when it was a proper music hall, and the other to the present after it has become a virtual ruin. To do this we built the theatre in its prime, decorated with shimmering gilt ornament and gas lamps, and filmed all the sequences relating to that period. Then we wrecked it, smashed the plasterwork and ripped up the seats until we had the right air of ultimate mournful decay.

Right, top: the auditorium in its distressed state, after we had trashed it to show the old music hall in its time of decay.

Right, below left: The theatre during construction, from which you can get an idea of its relatively huge scale for an animation film. Below right is the second proscenium arch where we filmed on-stage scenes to save time while the main auditorium was in use.

Set drawing for *Stage Fright*, the stalls and galleries filled with 80-90 characters. In some shots every one of them had to be animated, especially when they were applauding or jeering.

On the right is a plan view of the auditorium, showing the boxes near the stage which swung open like doors so that between shots the animators could move in and animate the characters.

It was a big set, measuring about 10ft (3m) from front to back, 6ft (1.8m) high and 6ft (1.8m) wide, and consisted of about thirty separate pieces. Fitting it all together was like doing a 3-D jigsaw puzzle. Along the side walls of the auditorium we had little boxes for members of the audience. We built these side parts as big doors which could be opened out on hinges. The animators could then go in, animate the figures in the audience, including those in the boxes, then close the door ready for the next shot. The hinges were disguised under architectural columns which looked like part of the theatre's design. We also built a second proscenium arch and front-stage area so we could film on-stage shots at the same time as the more complicated sequences were being photographed in the main theatre.

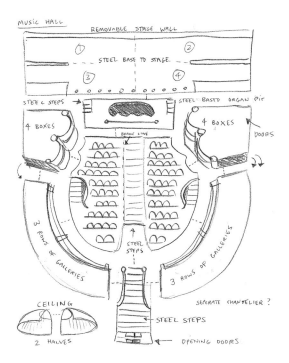

Below: The hand next to this display of Wallace's tool-kit gives an idea of how minute such props have to be. To compare the real-life scale of the saw in this group with the saw as it actually appears in the film frame, look at the picture on page 76.

Ingenuity and Props

Because we work in miniature, all our props are small. Some, however, are very small. Many of these are hand-held items - a toaster, a tea set, a hair-drier, a plate of burger and chips. All these things have to be made in the same scale as the hands that will hold or carry them, although that is not necessarily the same as the scale of the set. Hands are often made disproportionately large to cope with all the work they have to do, so if the same prop was held up to the character's head it would look ridiculous. To get over this, you probably have to make a smaller version of the prop. Close-ups, on the other hand, look better with a larger version. These are just some of the complications that our prop-makers have to bear in mind as they search for ingenious ways to convey the essence of an object. Over the years they acquire an extraordinary mental directory of solutions to cover anything from a tiny submarine to an electric fire that actually glows.

As ever, there are no fixed rules about materials or methods of construction. For fine or detailed work, prop-makers sometimes use rather finer materials than basic modelling clay. Products such as Fimo, Milliput and Sculpy are easier to model than standard Plasticine; the sculpted object can then be baked in an oven and hand-painted. Items of clothing are often sculpted in Plasticine, then a plaster mould is made and filled with latex which has lengths of wire inside it. If you want, for example, an apron or a coat that will flap in the wind, the wire helps it to hold its position. When several versions of the same prop are needed, such as shoes or hats, it may be best to use fast-cast resin and a silicone mould.

Graphic items such as newspapers or Wallace's travel and cheese magazines can usually be produced on the computer and reduced down. The same goes for posters, wall-signs and notices on shop-fronts. If a character needs to hold a newspaper while reading it, you can back the paper with heavy-duty foil to hold it firm while in shot. Household decorations, such as the pictures on the wall, the wallpaper and carpets in Wallace's living room are all hand-painted. You could make these by photocopying, but usually directors prefer things to have a home-made feel. We have also included a number of glass objects in our films. These are made for us by a professional glassblower.

A Moon rocket no taller than a paint-brush, from *A Grand Day Out,* and a flying toaster made for an episode of Morph.

Right: Gromit flies round on the end of a miniature power drill; from *A Grand Day Out.*

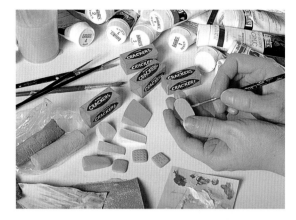

Prop-making for small worlds.

This page, from top: Making Wallace's favourite crackers, and the packets too.

Mocking up newspapers and other paper items. These may be needed for a character to hold and read, or for display in a newsagent's window, as shown. Newspaper props are backed with heavy-duty foil so they hold their position during shooting.

In the glassblower's workshop, where all manner of glass objects are made, including the milk bottles which feature at the end of the chase sequence in *The Wrong Trousers*.

Wallace's hair-drier with an action frame from *The Wrong Trousers*.

Opposite: A parade of objects to demonstrate the invention and artistry of the prop-makers. They include the submarine that journeyed through Vince's brain in the 'Rex the Runt' series, and the basket used by Tiny, the dog-juggler in *Stage Fright*.

Left to right: Ancient
exhibits from the museum
in *The Wrong Trousers;*
Contemporary table and
lamp from *Not Without My
Handbag;* fantastic creatures
from the *Rex the Runt* series,
an animated dustbin
featured in *Morph,* and tiny
instruments for Rex's band.
Though beautifully crafted,
some of these props were
only seen for a fleeting
second in the final film.

Miniature engineering from John Wright's workshop. Wallace's motor-bike is engineered like a real motor-bike, with welded parts and steel frames. Even the wheel spokes are individually stitched with wire and drilled into the wheel frame. The tyres are rubber, like real ones. Working parts such as the exhaust and engine are made of steel and chrome and heated to make them look scorched.

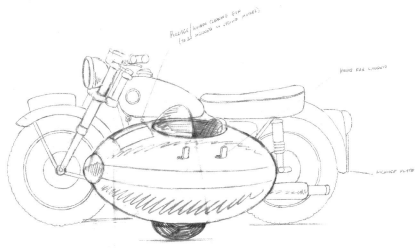

Big machines, like the Mutton-O-Matic, are made using foundry-cast brass parts. With such pieces, it is good to put everything on them, as for an all-round view, with all the rivets showing. When you are making the model, you never know which camera angle will finally be chosen.

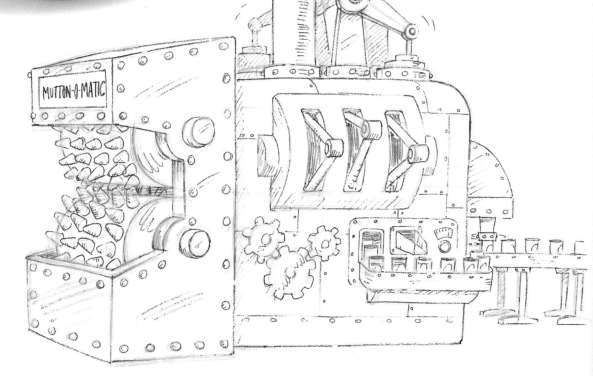

He's leaving home. For this rain scene in *The Wrong Trousers,* we superimposed live-action rain. The water running down Gromit's cape was actually tiny blobs of glycerine which were animated frame by frame.

Right: Ghost effect in *Stage Fright,* basically achieved by double exposure.

Special Effects

Some special effects are made principally with the camera. Others rely on physical factors such as the use of glass to lend invisible support, or artfully chosen props and materials which can be made to pass off as something else. Usually, though, a successful effect is a blend of both. How you light your scene is also important.

Double exposure For double exposures, or superimpositions, which can be applied to produce ghost effects, you need a camera with a windback facility. First, expose your main scene, then wind back the film by the number of frames in which you want your ghost to appear. If you then expose this figure against a black background, it will show through on

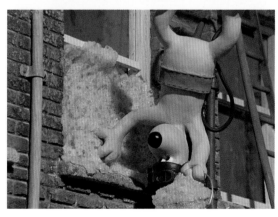

Top: The secret of pouring tea is to use rolls of squashed-up brown Cellophane. This catches the light and makes it look as if it is moving; from *Palmy Days.*

Centre: Beads of sweat fly off the anxious Penguin's brow in *The Wrong Trousers.* **The sweat was made by animating tiny perspex drops across the window in front of the character.**

Bottom: Washing windows with a foam of white hair wax dotted with different-sized glass beads; from *A Close Shave.* **As with all new solutions, once you have made the wonderful discovery that foam = white hair wax + added glass beads, you can apply the formula to other situations to make, say, shaving foam or bubble-bath.**

the first exposure and be transparent, like a ghost. Black velvet is best for the background, because it reflects less light than black paper. You can extend this trick to other kinds of apparition, as the Victorian photographers did with their scenes of 'The soldier's dream of his loved-ones' and 'The fairies' dell', etc.

Mattes The simplest form is the split screen. Here you mask off one side of the picture and shoot the action that fits into the unmasked half. You rewind the film, swap the mask over and shoot the action for the other side. This process can be further developed by using a sheet of glass in front of the camera, on which an area of the image is masked off with black paint - for example, the action to be seen inside the windows of a miniature space-ship. The ship is shot with the window areas painted out on the glass. Then the film is rewound, the clear area painted black and the previously painted area scraped clear, and finally the action for the window is set up in front of the camera and shot.

Water and rain effects Water and other liquids are difficult to simulate, and animators have tried out various ways to convey the illusion. A classic method for flat water, say a lake or river, is to cut a perspex sheet to size and spray it with the colours you want, adding ripple effects and so on.

For the rain effect in *The Wrong Trousers,* we put little blobs of glycerine on glass and animated them by blowing them, frame by frame, down the glass. Then, every so often, we put in a random splash effect, a tiny winged object that looked like a very small butterfly and was made out of cel. We stuck this on Gromit's raincoat and on the ground, just for one frame, then took it off. In another scene in *The Wrong Trousers,* the Penguin is outside the museum window during the robbery, and beads of sweat fly off him. Again, we animated small perspex drops across the glass away from him. For the foam in the window-washing sequence in *A Close Shave,* we came up with a combination of white hair wax dotted with glass beads to represent the bubbles. To suggest bubbles bursting and new ones forming, we took beads out and put in new ones.

Advanced Special Effects

There are some special effects you cannot easily achieve with model animation. For example, it is difficult to convey the illusion of high-speed motion. If you animate objects moving fast across the screen, you often get jerky, 'strobing' movement because the distance between the positions of the models from one frame to another is too great for the brain to smooth out. The problem is exacerbated by the sharp images created by photographing static objects.

When shot as live-action film, fast-moving objects create a blurred image on each frame of the film because they are moving during the relatively long exposure made by the live-action camera. These blurred, indistinct images are more easily smoothed over by the brain than the hard-edged, sharp images

Left: The train chase scene in *The Wrong Trousers.* **By moving the train and the camera together during a two-second exposure, it and the characters on board come out sharply defined, whereas the wallpaper background is blurred.**

created by stop-frame animation. To avoid the jerky effects of fast-moving objects in animation, you have to create blurred images. In the train chase in *The Wrong Trousers* and the lorry chase in *A Close Shave,* we blurred the background by using long exposures (one or two seconds) and by physically moving the camera during the exposure.

To take the train example, the train on its track was attached to the camera, which was mounted on a dolly. For each frame, we pushed the dolly about 3-4in (8-10cm) and this carried the train along with it. At the same time we pressed the button to expose the film. The characters on the train come out sharply defined because they are moving with the camera, but in the course of the two-second exposure the camera moves fractionally past the wallpaper in the background, and this comes out blurred.

Blue-screen This process is used a great deal in films today. It is a way of putting difficult foreground action against a realistic background - for example, to show people falling out of a building. We use the technique frequently when we want to put animated characters into a live-action background. First, the foreground action (the people falling) is shot against a blue background. The blue is then electronically replaced by the chosen background (the building) using a sophisticated computer graphics system (it used to be done in the film laboratories, but this is rare nowadays). This has the effect of merging the two elements of the scene. Naturally, you have to be careful to match the lighting, perspective and camera angles, otherwise it can look like cut-out images stuck on another picture!

Douglas the Lurpak Butter man, filmed by the blue-screen process. First he is shot against a blue background, then the blue is electronically replaced by the table-top scene. We use blue as the background colour because human faces do not usually have much blue in them. Any strong colour will do, such as lime green, but it is important to ensure that the colour does not appear in the surrounding scene because it will also be removed in the process.

animation and performance

Movement

Like actors, animators communicate through the language of movement. We create characters, convey emotions and make people laugh through the movements, gestures and facial expressions of our puppets.

People often say that our work is naturalistic, which I think is meant as a compliment because the best model animation is regularly praised for its

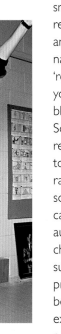

smooth and 'natural' movement. But in fact our work is not realistic at all. It is - and it should be - exaggerated. All the animated movements that we do, however understated or natural they may appear, are bigger, bolder and simpler than 'real life'. Real movement, the sort of thing you would see if you analysed film of a live actor, always looks weak and bland when it is closely imitated in an animated version. Some animators use previously shot live-action footage as reference material, or even copy it slavishly frame by frame to create their own animated performance. At Aardman we rarely do this. We prefer to act out the animation ourselves, so that we really understand it, then add our own degree of caricature and stylisation. The important thing is that the audience should be able to understand what the puppet character is doing and thinking, no matter how broad or subtle the style of animation. What we love doing is producing *performances* with our puppets that feel 'natural' because in some way they feel true. By simplifying and exaggerating gestures, we try to distil the essence of a particular movement or sequence of movements. This is far more important than copying from real life. When we get this right, it gives the audience a great sense of recognition. They think, 'Yes, that's exactly how people react or behave,' and they believe that what they have seen is uncannily natural.

Nick Park, stopwatch in hand, uses his own body to work through the jerky, exaggerated movements of the Wrong Trousers (seen right in action). Once he knows exactly how long it takes to get from A to B in a particular phase, he can plan how to animate the model within this timespan.

Posing the Character

Obviously, animation is about movement. But few really expressive sequences are carried out through *continuous* movement. One of the classic symptoms of our earliest work is that the characters shift about constantly and restlesslessly, never daring to be still. Later we realised that the time between movements, when the puppet is still, often conveys far more character than the same number of seconds of elaborate animation.

We talk of 'poses' and 'holds'. A pose is pretty obvious - a still position that conveys a lot of information about mood and emotion. A hold is the moment when the action stops - though it seldom freezes completely - and it can last for anything from a quarter of a second to half a minute. During these holds, the audience can see and understand far more than when the character is continually moving. The point to remember is that your puppet is never *just* sitting or standing or leaning - it should always be expressive in face and body. You should always know what your character is thinking and feeling - if you don't, who does? - and in the poses, you make it clear to the audience.

To be sure, I certainly do not mean that the pose has to be like some magnificent melodramatic gesture from a Victorian painting. Audiences are very sophisticated, and the pose can be as subtle, or as corny, as you can make it. If your puppet is frightened, he does not have to be cringing and quaking in extravagant terror. The fear can be communicated in the angle of the head, the tension in the shoulders and arms and the smallest obsessive gesture with one hand.

Remember that these holds should not be totally static. Watch television with the sound off, or watch people in the street. You often see people sit or stand for several minutes at a time, doing virtually nothing. However, they are moving in slight ways, and they *are* alive. If your puppet goes into a hold, keep it alive, don't let it freeze, and look on this as an opportunity to let the audience see what he or she is thinking and feeling.

Changing the Pace Of course, different actions happen at different speeds. Building a house of cards is a slow and careful business, whereas trying to extract a lighted cigarette from inside your clothing is going to be pretty frenetic. But whatever the speed of the sequence, try to vary the pace of individual parts of your animation. Try to avoid falling into a too-regular rhythm of move-hold-move-hold. Remember too that different parts of the body can move at different speeds. A thief may creep carefully through an empty house, but his head and eyes can move quickly and sharply.

★ **In the animated sequences on the following pages, we show key frames to illustrate the essence of a movement. In a full sequence, there would be other, intervening frames.**

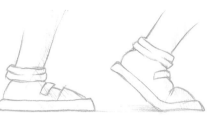

When a hand or a foot - or a bottom or a nose - comes into contact with the ground, make it look as if it is firmly set. Make it lie flat and contact the ground at all points, so that no line of light is visible underneath. This makes the puppet feel larger and heavier.

Remember that your puppet has a centre of gravity, and needs to stay well balanced. Standing with his weight equally on both feet, you want him to step forward on to his right foot. To do this, he must first shift his body weight over his supporting foot, the left. The best demonstration is to try it yourself. Start with your feet very close together, and step forward on to your right foot. As you start, you move very slightly to the left. Starting with your feet a metre apart, you are forced to move a long way to the left before you can go forward. Now try moving off without shifting left and see how unnatural it feels.

Right: Everything about this puppet is downcast. His feet barely leave the ground, his head bounces slowly as if he has not got the strength to hold it up, and his arms swing heavily in small arcs.

Every step we take starts at the hip joint. Your puppet should do the same. When he prepares to move off, the supporting hip drops down as the body's weight is transferred on to it. The pelvis swivels and the stepping foot is released.

Walk Cycles in Action

Adam
Adam is so dejected, his whole body hangs heavily. As he plods slowly uphill, his arms barely swing.

Wallace
The Wrong Trousers take Wallace for a walk. The trousers move with an extreme mechanical step, which causes Wallace's hands and head to wave about in panic.

Loves Me ... Loves Me Not
As the puppet tangoes across the floor, his legs smooth out the action like shock absorbers.

Wat
In most 'real' walks, the head is kept quite still. In this scene Wat moves with exaggerated effort and his head bobs up and down wearily.

Substitution
The substitution technique allows us to create lovely smooth lines in the legs and feet, and gives extra stretch as the front foot reaches forward.

Making Movement Believable

Anticipation Before an animated figure starts moving in one direction, we usually anticipate the action by moving it the opposite way. This is not so strange when you think about it. If you want to jump up in the air, you first crouch down; if you want to throw a ball forward, the first thing your arm does is go back. Anticipation is 'realistic', and it also works well in film because the moment of anticipation prepares the audience for the action which is going to follow. This is why, in cartoon films, the anticipation is often stronger than the action itself.

Weight We make our characters more believable by making them look heavy. The weightlifter, above, nicely demonstrates this as he struggles to lift a barbell which only weighs a couple of ounces. The animator plans and rehearses the movement, miming it to understand how it works. Then he tries to make the puppet do the hard work. In stage 3 for example, he has just started to lift by pushing his legs and back straight, and stretching his arms. At stage 4, he has hauled the barbell as high as he can, it hangs in the air for a moment before it

Above: Think about the weightlifter's speed through the lift. Most of the action is quite slow, but at stage 4 he suddenly snatches up the weight, and at 5 he quickly gets his hands and arms below the barbell.

Top: Wallace walks across the museum ceiling in *The Wrong Trousers,* his leg movements controlled by Feathers McGraw from outside the window. The way he moves reflects both the character and his plight. The Penguin, mindful of the risks he is taking, moves the Trousers with exaggerated care. The knees come up high and the feet are planted with great caution, to make sure they stick. Inside the Trousers, Wallace moves to a linked but different pattern.

falls, and in that time he quickly gets his hands and body underneath it. When he finally holds the weight aloft in triumph, see how his arms and legs are locked straight. If they were not, the audience would not believe he could support a heavy weight.

Momentum Remember that, like the barbell, your head, body and limbs are also heavy. Because of this, they should not stop moving too quickly once they start. Try sprinting as fast as you can, then stopping. When your feet finally stop, thanks to friction, your head and body will want to carry on, tipping you forward. In animation, we often exaggerate this natural effect.

Acceleration and Deceleration Except in extreme cases, objects and people do not suddenly start or stop moving at full speed. They normally accelerate and decelerate. This is pretty obvious in the case of a sprinter running from the starting blocks, but it applies equally to small actions such as lifting your hand to scratch your ear. Remember that your hand and arm have weight, and have to be brought up to speed.

See how his arms swing like a pendulum, but always behind the movement of the feet. When a foot is forward, the arms swing helplessly back, then swing forward again as the next stride begins.

Very little human movement happens in straight lines. It can usually be broken down into a series of arcs. If you trace the path of the batter's foot, hand or hip, you should see a pattern of overlapping curves.

Putting it all together

The sequences here show a mix of all the animation principles mentioned in the previous pages. Swinging a baseball bat is a good example because the whole process is about storing up and using energy.

Stage 1 shows the batter poised to receive the ball. In 2 and 3 he moves back, anticipating the main action which will be forward. His shoulders rotate, storing energy, and his weight is entirely on the back foot, allowing him to raise the left

All the sequences on these pages demonstrate how movement flows through a gesture. I think of it as a wave that runs through the body from the first thing that moves to the last. Swinging the bat starts when the foot steps forward, followed by the knee, hip, chest, shoulder, elbow, hand and finally the bat.

Right: The force of the flying ball catches the man's hand and pulls him along in a sequence that runs from his hand down to his feet.

foot. He steps forward on to his front foot, and by 5 has started to unwind his shoulders. As he accelerates, the bat moves a greater distance in each frame.

The bat has weight and is swinging in a big arc, so in 6 and 7 it is moving farther than anything else. All his weight is pushing on to the front foot, and his whole body is unwinding so that maximum force and speed are brought to bear on the ball at stage 7. At 8, the power which started in the hips and shoulders has now been transferred to the bat which is almost pulling him round in his follow-through. In a more 'cartoony' version, his bat would carry on and get wrapped round behind his head.

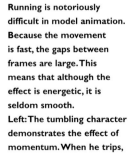

Running is notoriously difficult in model animation. Because the movement is fast, the gaps between frames are large. This means that although the effect is energetic, it is seldom smooth.

Left: The tumbling character demonstrates the effect of momentum. When he trips, his feet stop moving but his head keeps going forward (4). In turn, his tumbling body pulls his feet after him (6). When his head contacts the ground, the feet - still full of energy - carry on past (7) until they finally settle on the ground (8). If he was running faster, he would carry on tumbling longer.

Action and Reaction

Porridge Power
The impact of the flying blob of porridge knocks Wallace back in his chair. Just as he recovers to an upright position, the action is repeated.

Pib Shoots Pog
Pib reels back from the recoil of the gun and Pog under the force of the projectile. They sway back into an upright stance, and Pog turns to reveal a very large bullet hole.

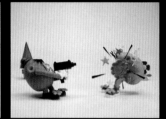

Carpet Trick
The boy's whirling legs ruck the carpet into extravagantly huge ridges. In classic cartoon style, when his legs touch the ground, they zoom off first, followed a moment later by the body and head.

Bungee Effect
Gromit's legs, helmet and bucket tell the story. In frame 3, when his body has stopped falling, his legs are the last things to stop. When he finds himself pulled up again (6), his legs are the last thing to start moving.

Adam Takes Strike
A study in anticipation as Adam coils himself up to strike. See how in frame 7 he has started to unwind into the stroke from his foot to the shoulder, but the pack is still in a state of anticipation - it has not yet moved.

Special Movement Effects

We are often asked how the Penguin got into the bottle in *The Wrong Trousers*. In fact this was a relatively straightforward thing to do, relying on a quick substitution of both character and bottle. The sequence, illustrated below, begins with the empty milk bottle wobbling and vibrating after Gromit has crashed into the cupboard. Then it falls off the unit and Gromit catches it. Up till then we used an ordinary model bottle. For the next frames we had a thin replacement Penguin who is first seen entering the bottle before he becomes inescapably jammed up to the neck inside it. This was a different bottle, vacuum-formed and supplied in two halves. We pushed the thin clay Penguin against the side of one half and then sealed him in, hiding the join when we positioned the bottle to camera.

Another difficult part of this sequence was animating the Penguin after he has been shot up in the air and then falls to earth against a background of sky and clouds. Rather than try to show the Penguin in motion against a fixed background, we photographed him on glass with a parallel sky positioned behind him. In the following frames the Penguin is largely still, though from time to time we altered the position of his feet and the sack across his shoulder. The illusion of falling comes mainly from the sky itself, which we moved from side to side during a series of long exposures. This was a variant on the blurred-wallpaper effect which occurs earlier in the train chase (described on page 127).

Again, while shooting *Adam,* we had to go to great lengths of ingenuity to show him running round the circumference of the world. For most of the film, Adam stands on top of his globe, which was supported on the end of a scaffolding pole. This was fixed through the far side of the globe and so always remained out of shot. The pole also ran through a hole in the night-sky picture which was our backdrop. For the running sequence, it would have been incredibly painful to animate Adam by holding him on strings and changing their position after each shot, so we came up with another solution.

First we turned the globe-pole-sky unit on its side, through 90 degrees. Then we measured the circumference of the globe and cut a circular hole in a large

The Penguin falls to earth in *The Wrong Trousers*. The illusion of falling was mainly achieved by pulling the painted background from side to side during a series of long exposures.

How the Penguin got into the bottle. This was a two-bottle and two-Penguin trick. When the Penguin began entering the bottle, his body was exchanged for a special thin Penguin. The receiving bottle was also different - it came in two halves and was clamped round the Penguin between shots.

When Adam ran round the circumference of the globe, we shot him on glass. With one hip and one shoulder resting against the glass, he was far easier to animate than if we had tried somehow to suspend him on wires.

sheet of glass which fitted exactly round the globe on a north-south axis. So now, because everything was turned, we had the camera up in the roof shooting downward. After that, it was relatively easy to film Adam running round the world because he was lying with one shoulder and one hip flat on the glass.

If you should try something like that yourself, there are two snags: extra colour from the glass, and reflections. A sheet of glass may have some colour in it, and this is likely to show up when you move from the previous scene, which has no glass in it, into your with-glass scene, and similarly when you move out of it into the next scene. To avoid this, shoot a whole group of scenes with a sheet of glass in them, whether they need it or not, and the transition will not show up. To avoid picking up reflections thrown by the puppet lying on its side, shoot directly at 90 degrees to the glass. There may still be some reflection, but this should be minimal.

Arnold, the bully figure from
Stage Fright, **and some of the**
replacement mouths that
helped to keep fame and
fortune at a distance in his
career as an entertainer.

His short pointy teeth, allied
to fierce eyes and alarming
carroty hair, give him a
powerful expressive range.
Think of this when deciding
on the kind of facial effects
you want your character
to produce.

Expressions and Gestures

Although we spend a lot of time on mouths, working with dope sheets to synchronise speech and mouth movements (see pages 150-151), and yet more time making this work by constantly sculpting and resculpting mouths, or fitting replacement mouths, this part of the face is by no means the most expressive. The mouth is of course crucial to speech, but perhaps supplies only 5-10 per cent of a character's performance.

Those moments that really make you believe that this clay person is talking are all done with the eyes, eyebrows and gestures involving the face - nods, nose-scratching, stroking the cheek while thinking something over, and so on. Bear in mind, too, that a character can be highly expressive without speaking a single word. Gromit is a good example of this: almost all his expressiveness comes from the way his eyes are positioned. Many of our models' eyes are made of glass beads with a painted-on pupil, which has a hole at its centre. To move the eyes around, and make them look up, down or sideways, the animator inserts a cocktail stick into the hole in the pupil and swivels the eye to the desired position. Eyebrows are used to enhance certain facial expressions - surprise, for example - and eyelids, often made of fast-cast resin, are added if the character is required to blink, fall asleep or wake up.

Hand and arm gestures are also important in their own right, whether they involve touching the face or not. The amount they can be used will naturally depend on the build of the character. As Nick Park found while making *Creature Comforts,* not all animals are designed with the kind of front paws that can be waved about expressively: 'It was fine for the Jaguar and the Polar Bears, because they had these front legs and paws, but some animals did not have anything I could work with. The young Hippopotamus just had two cloven front hooves, which he needed to support himself while sitting up, and the Armadillo was even more limited. With the Bush Baby, it was enough to have her clinging on to the branch to bring out her insecurity. I also made her lift her glasses off, so people could see those two little timid eyes beneath.'

★ **Clay faces and hands get**
dirty very quickly. The best
way to clean them is very
gently to scrape off the top
layer. The important thing is
to keep a constant balance
between the tones of a
model's face and any separate
pieces, such as mouths and
eyelids, that you may fix to it.

The more you scrape away,
the more you have to add new
bits of clay, and here too you
can get differences in tone.
Eventually, you reach a stage
where you cannot get the dirt
out of the face, and then you
have to make a new one.

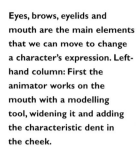

Eyes, brows, eyelids and mouth are the main elements that we can move to change a character's expression. Left-hand column: First the animator works on the mouth with a modelling tool, widening it and adding the characteristic dent in the cheek.

The eyes are turned by inserting a cocktail stick in the pre-drilled hole at the centre of the pupil and swivelling the eye (in reality a glass bead) to the required position.

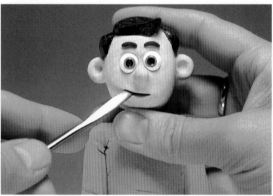

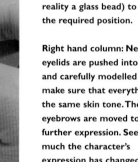

Right hand column: Next the eyelids are pushed into place and carefully modelled in to make sure that everything has the same skin tone. The eyebrows are moved to create further expression. See how much the character's expression has changed since the first frame.

Faces and Expressions

In *Going Equipped,*
the characterisation
is exaggerated but
basically realistic.

Gromit shows expression
through his eyes and
particularly through Nick
Park's trademark animated
brow - from inquiry to
determination to despair.

Dark moods and uncertainty
in the faces of the stars of
Stage Fright.

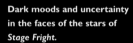

Pib and Pog accompany the
extreme violence of their
actions with obvious,
'cartoony' facial expressions
to show, as here, perplexity,
sly triumph, dismay and
wicked glee.

Right and opposite: Sprawled
across his tree perch, the
Jaguar is free to gesture
massively at the unreasonable
fate which has befallen him.

Lip Sync

We match voices to lip movements by a somewhat ancient method which has become traditional in the company. First, an editor marks all the syllables on the magnetic tape of the dialogue recording. Then he or she transfers all this to a bar chart, in which each bar covers a second of film (or 1ft of 35mm), so the animator can see exactly where each syllable starts and finishes. With the word 'Me', for example, the chart will show the 'M'-sound lasting for two frames, or whatever, and the longer 'eeeee' sound lasting for nine frames. If there is pre-recorded music, as there might be for a film which is set round a tune or song, this will also be sketched in, to show where the beats fall, or a particular run of notes which are important for the animator's timing.

The chart goes to the animator, who then copies the information on to a traditional animation dope sheet. There are 96 lines to a page, one line for each frame, covering 4 seconds, and the lines run vertically down the sheet. On the dope sheet you have more space to put other information, and that is the essential difference. Instead of having just a tiny gap per frame, as on the bar chart, here the animator has a whole line.

Now you have your own personal map of the sounds, and the gaps between them, and can begin to devise a performance for your character. From listening to the sound, you know when the voice goes up higher - which might indicate a questioning expression, with raised eyebrows. In *War Story*, the old man says

Nick Park and Steve Box prepare Wendolene for her next scene in *A Close Shave*, matching gesture to storyboard.

Below is a chart of Wendolene sounds, each one pinpointing the position of the mouth.

Opposite, below, is a sample dope sheet, which provides the animator with an accurate map of the sounds a character will make, and how many frames each one will occupy. This is matched, top, with the face the audience sees while hearing the sounds on the soundtrack.

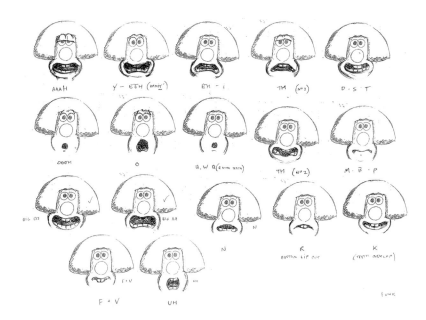

to his interviewer, 'I was out at the BAC, see, Pete?' You listen to that, and try to work out when he should raise his eyebrows, or tilt his head. Typically you listen over and over again, repeating it to yourself, copying the accent and intonation, trying to sense the right moment for the character to react. You can hear that he pauses after 'BAC', so you choose that as the moment. The dope sheet, meanwhile, tells you the exact space between 'C' and 'see' is 18 frames. This is the essential information you need both to plan ahead, and to animate.

How much an animator actually notes down on the dope sheet is a matter of personal choice. You could write down every detail, but with experience you tend to write less. Alongside our sample piece of speech, you might mark in certain movements, e.g. 'blink ... blink ... starts to raise hand to face - 18 frames (during that time, starts to tilt head to left) . . . tilts head to left - 12 frames'. And so on. Sometimes it can be deadening to analyse a movement too closely, fragment by fragment. Today I tend to write down just the key moments, where the timing is essential, and leave the rest to inspiration when we shoot. On the other hand, some gestures are so specific that it can be helpful to note down all the separate movements, of hands, eyebrows, angle of head, etc., to make sure you include them all and that they blend together.

One important tip is to look ahead at all times. It is too easy to develop a kind of tunnel vision with the frame you are working on, and then you can forget to start another movement in time, or you find that your character is out of position and cannot make the expressive move you want him to.

As for marrying the sounds to lip movements, a character can either have its own set of replacement mouths, each corresponding to a particular sound or group of sounds, or you can decide to resculpt the face itself each frame - what we call 'animating through'. Even with replacement mouths, you still have to do a certain amount of remodelling to clean up the face and sculpt in the new mouth so it fits perfectly.

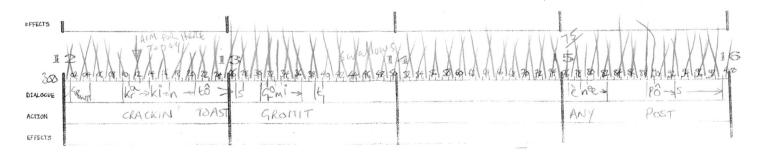

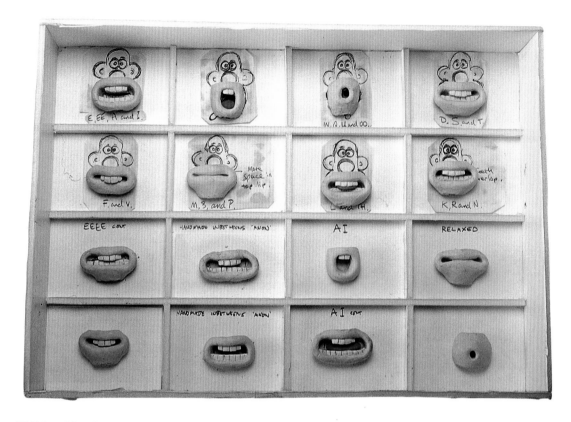

A box of Wallace's mouths, showing some of the sounds and expressions he can make with them, including the all-important 'relaxed' when he does not say anything at all or goes into listening mode.

Talking Heads

The idea of making up a set of replacement mouths for a character was conceived as a way of saving time. Because everything in animation takes so long, any time-saving device is to be welcomed. In theory, it should be quicker for the animator just to exchange one mouth for another, model it in to make sure the joins do not show, and shoot the next frame. Also, a replacement mouth has the advantage that it can be used a number of times, whereas if you reanimate a fixed mouth you lose that advantage. For all that, some animators still prefer the old-fashioned way, finding it more satisfactory to work with a head that remains a unified entity, and probably has less variation in skin tone, than with something that always consists of two halves that have to be constantly reunited.

Whichever way you choose, you have to be prepared to do a lot of cleaning and remodelling. If you have a mouth which you will only need for two or three frames, then this is not so important. But if it is a mouth you are going to use when the face comes to rest, and will be needed for a long sequence of frames, then you have to be sure that it is clean and that it tones in with the face.

The best cleaning liquid for clay is water. You can try lighter fluid, but this tends to strip away the whole surface of the face, leaving it sticky and more difficult to handle. For the best results, use water and gently scrape away at those parts you want to clean or remove.

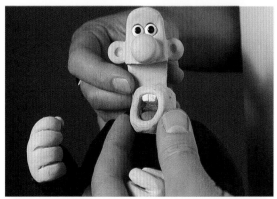

In this sequence, Wallace's 'ee' mouth is taken off and the new mouth which says 'o' is slid into place. The animator uses a modelling tool to mask the join and smooth down the new face.

making a film

Thinking about a Script

Whole stories do not fall ready-made from the sky. The best ones usually evolve slowly and take a huge amount of effort. Dave and I learned our trade in storytelling when we made films for 'Vision On' and 'Take Hart'. Those early films were very short - no more than sketches, really - but many of the same basic rules that we discovered then, apply equally to much longer and more complicated stories.

A story is usually about something, meaning that there is more to the story than simply what happens. Morph stories are usually about sibling rivalry, jealousy, pomposity pricked - things like that. But the seed from which the story grows may be very simple. It may be enough to think of a single gag, an absurd situation, an animation idea that you would love to try.

Morph, Chas and a keyboard - all the ingredients you need for a short sharp conflict. When we began making Morph films for the 'Vision On' series, our goal was to tell a story in under a minute - not a bad target for anyone setting out in animation.

When we were writing sketches for Morph, we had the freedom to choose any subject. For example, we might decide it would be fun to animate him as if he were on ice. That is not a story, but it is the seed from which the story grows. It is a situation that will be fun to do and will challenge the character. Now we need to work out how to simulate ice on Morph's table-top. He could invent an ice-making machine, or receive one through the post, like Wile E Coyote, or we could send him to the North Pole. Or we might decide that all this is much too complicated. Instead, Morph's alter ego Chas has polished the floor so hard that it becomes as slippery as ice. But Chas, being incredibly lazy, would never have polished the floor voluntarily. So he needs a reason that is funny and in character. The simplest reason is good old malice. Chas has booby-trapped the floor, and now lies in wait to watch the fun. Starting with an animation idea, a story is already forming.

All this is the set-up for the main part of the story, in which Morph tries to achieve something, and is constantly thwarted by the slippery floor. I am shy of giving rules, but we often found that you had to try three variations on a predicament to make it effective. In this case, discovering the slippery floor and falling over a few times is not enough. You have to invent *variations* on him falling over. Why does he do it, how does he avoid it, what are the consequences? And while he is falling over, while he is in conflict with Chas, we must not forget to have visual fun with Morph skating around. Finally, we need a punchline, an ending, a resolution. Knowing Morph, he eventually discovers that Chas is responsible and takes some terrible kind of revenge which leaves the audience with a feeling that justice has been done.

Nick Park and I think chickens - devising the shape, look and individual characteristics of the stars of their new feature film.

On a much bigger scale, the idea for *Wat's Pig* came during a holiday in France. I was in the Dordogne, where you can see these huge medieval castles standing in full view of one another. I thought, how difficult to have been a peasant in the middle of this lot, caught up in the intrigues of warring barons who held the key to everything you did in life. That was the starting-point. As we developed our plot, we settled on one particular castle rather than have two facing each other. Later came the idea of the twins who were separated by a thief who stole one of them. After that began the real job of knocking it all into a complete story, which took months of work.

Story-writing is like solving a great puzzle made up of dozens of elements. Think of Rubik's Cube. You twist the sides around to see if a given combination will work, then you twist it again, and again, until it comes out right. Along the way, you probably have to discard a few things as well, and that can be the hardest part.

Creating a Storyboard for *Adam*

With only one location, two characters and no dialogue, *Adam* is a very simple film. Even so, storyboarding it was not easy. At the ideas stage, I had come up with a dozen or more situations that Adam would face - the effect of gravity, loneliness, a temper tantrum, etc. The job was then to put the sequences in the best order. so that the story unfolded in the right way to an audience. I drew up each short sequence very swiftly and roughly - to capture the ideas in my head. Then, with hundreds of scratchy little drawings on separate sheets of paper, it was easy to shuffle them around to try out different ways of structuring the film. The storyboard drawings did not need to convey anything to anybody else about the look of the film. What they did convey to me was the spirit of each sequence, and also whether or not a gag was working.

So, along with body posture and facial expression, the most important thing the storyboard told me was the size and shape of the shot. Is loneliness conveyed better in a soulful close-up, or in a wide shot which shows that there is nobody and nothing else around? Or both? And in which order? It seems to me that such questions - half artistic and half practical - are the main business of storyboarding.

Peter Lord, seen on the right animating his character Adam, planned the film by drawing up the main sequences in a series of rough sketches like those shown below. By shuffling these around, he was able to organise the film's structure, and also check whether he had captured the spirit of each individual sequence.

Nick Park and Steve Box plan the scene where Gromit hides in a cardboard box to spy on the Penguin, and carves out a viewing slot like a pair of binoculars. On the wall, the storyboard shows the view from inside the box and from the Penguin's vantage point.
Right: Character sketches by Nick Park.

Creating a Storyboard for *The Wrong Trousers*

The storyboard can be a very exciting stage, the place where a film starts to come to fruition after all the preliminary work. Usually, one drawn storyboard picture represents one event in a shot. Some shots may contain two or three events, and if so we represent them all. We prepare the storyboard piece by piece, or scene by scene, then pin the sections on the wall to see how they fit together. The act of drawing the frames really helps you to grasp the story and get it into your head.

Sc.65. Shot 3. INT. DINING ROOM. NIGHT.

GROMIT CROSSES PENGUINS TRACK.

PENGUIN ABOUT TO COLLIDE WITH TRAIN.

Sc.65. Shot 3 continued,

WALLACE TRIES TO GRAB PENGUIN,..

Sc.65. Shot 3 continued,

...BUT PENGUIN TRUNDLES ON ENGINELESS.

Sc.65. Shot 4. INT. DINING ROOM. NIGHT.

WALLACE HAS GRABBED THE ENGINE

TRACKING SHOT.

Sc.65. Shot 5. INT. DINING ROOM. NIGHT.

GROMITS TRAIN CURVES AROUND TO COME
UP PARALLEL TO PENGUINS TRACK.
GROMIT RUNS OUT OF TRACK AND DISCARDS
THE BOX.   TRACK WITH PENGUIN.

Sc.65. Shot 6. INT. DINING ROOM. NIGHT.

PENGUINS P.O.V. TROUSERS STEP ON HIS
TRACK. (WE'RE HEADING FOR KITCHEN)

TRACKING SHOT.

Sc.65. Shot 7. INT. DINING ROOM. NIGHT.

PANICKED PENGUIN TRIES TO BRAKE AND
WALLACE AND GROMIT OVERTAKE.

TRACKING SHOT.

Sc.65. Shot 7. continued.

TROUSER FOOT COMES DOWN ON THE TRACK.
PENGUIN GOES FLYING.

Sc.66. Shot 1. INT. KITCHEN. NIGHT.

WALLACE REACHES UP TO GRAB PENGUIN.

TRACKING SHOT

Sc.66. Shot 2. INT. KITCHEN. NIGHT.

GROMIT ANTICIPATES A CATCH.

TRACKING SHOT.

PENGUIN SAILS THROUGH THE AIR.

TRACKING SHOT.

Sc.66. Shot 4. INT. KITCHEN. NIGHT.

GROMIT SMASHES INTO KITCHEN UNIT CUPBOARDS.

TRACK THEN STOP.

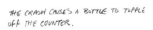

Sc.66. Shot 5. INT. KITCHEN. NIGHT.

THE CRASH CAUSES A BOTTLE TO TOPPLE
OFF THE COUNTER.

Sc.66. Shot 6. INT. KITCHEN. NIGHT.

PENGUIN DESCENDS TRY TO FLY? ONE
WING.

Sc.66. Shot 7. INT. KITCHEN. NIGHT.

BOTTLE LANDS IN GROMIT LAP....

Sc.66. Shot 7 continued.

..PERFECTLY POSITIONED TO CATCH THE
PENGUIN AND THE DIAMOND.
"ATTABOY GROMIT LAD!

Sc.66. Shot 8. INT. KITCHEN. NIGHT.

WALLACE SLIDES INTO FRAME:
"WELL DONE! WE DID IT!"

Nick Park: 'This sequence in *The Wrong Trousers* was the first one we storyboarded. Even before we started writing the script, I storyboarded this whole sequence - and we stuck with it. Sometimes scenes change a lot, either when we shoot or in the cutting room, or they may be dropped entirely, but we managed to keep this one. It was edited down quite a lot, but the essence of the storyboard is still there.'

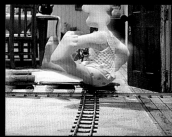

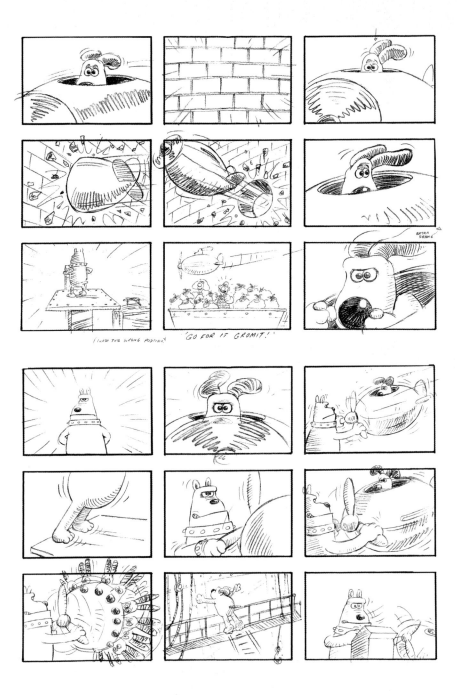

Creating a Storyboard for *A Close Shave*

Nick Park: 'We had less time to storyboard this film, so we tended to skip events and represent the shot in just one frame. I roughed out what we wanted and then Michael Salter, who was working with me, drew up the frames more elaborately. With most films we do the storyboard after the script has been written, so we already have a clear view of what we are going to do. The storyboard helps us to refine that view and put the words into a coherent visual form.'

The storyboard frames show Gromit flying in to attack Preston. In the completed version, right, he then opens fire with the porridge gun before Preston manages to get his paws on the propeller.

Characterisation - Morph

When Dave and I brought Morph into the BBC series 'Take Hart', he was not much more than a human-shaped blob. The challenge for us was to develop him into a fully-fledged character.

Back in 'Vision On' days, we had created a group of little clay characters, called the Gleebies, who ran round the tabletop and created havoc, knocking over paint pots and stuff like that. The producer liked them, and when he was preparing the 'Take Hart' series he asked us to create a new character who could interact with the artist Tony Hart, and who would apparently live in his studio. He also liked the fact that our plasticine characters could change shape. So we made a very simple terracotta-coloured figure who could instantly change back into a lump of plasticine. Because he could metamorphose, we called him Morph. The problem then was to find things for him to do.

Morph was a troublemaker from day one, and from that came his personality. He was disrespectful of authority, viz Tony Hart, and gradually, story by story, he acquired more and more characteristics. In each episode we set him a problem to solve, and the way he reacted to it gave him another dimension. We also decided to cut down on the amount he changed shape, because that did not interest us as much as his character.

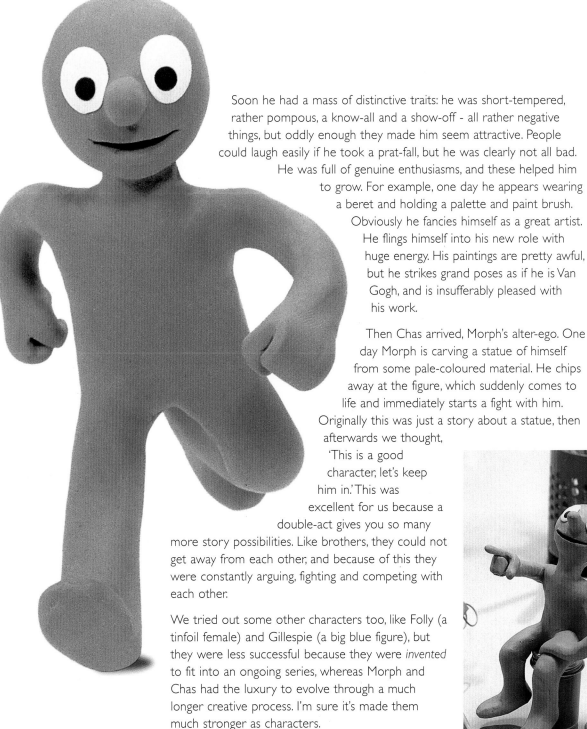

Soon he had a mass of distinctive traits: he was short-tempered, rather pompous, a know-all and a show-off - all rather negative things, but oddly enough they made him seem attractive. People could laugh easily if he took a prat-fall, but he was clearly not all bad. He was full of genuine enthusiasms, and these helped him to grow. For example, one day he appears wearing a beret and holding a palette and paint brush. Obviously he fancies himself as a great artist. He flings himself into his new role with huge energy. His paintings are pretty awful, but he strikes grand poses as if he is Van Gogh, and is insufferably pleased with his work.

Then Chas arrived, Morph's alter-ego. One day Morph is carving a statue of himself from some pale-coloured material. He chips away at the figure, which suddenly comes to life and immediately starts a fight with him. Originally this was just a story about a statue, then afterwards we thought, 'This is a good character, let's keep him in.' This was excellent for us because a double-act gives you so many more story possibilities. Like brothers, they could not get away from each other, and because of this they were constantly arguing, fighting and competing with each other.

We tried out some other characters too, like Folly (a tinfoil female) and Gillespie (a big blue figure), but they were less successful because they were *invented* to fit into an ongoing series, whereas Morph and Chas had the luxury to evolve through a much longer creative process. I'm sure it's made them much stronger as characters.

On these pages Morph displays some of his many characteristics. On the plus side, he is friendly and full of genuine enthusiasms. Less positively, he is pompous and definitely likes to get his own way, especially with Chas, the brother-figure he cannot stop arguing and fighting with.

Characterisation - *Creature Comforts*

The action takes place in a zoo where the animal characters - a Jaguar, a Gorilla, a Terrapin, three Polar Bears and others - talk about their lives and how they are treated. The film won director Nick Park his first Oscar. Here he discusses the characters and how he developed them.

The title frame of *Creature Comforts* shows a professional tape recorder. A voice says, 'Sound running. When you're ready'. This sets up the film as a series of interviews, and conveys to the viewer that the voices in the film are 'real'.

'The idea came from what Pete and Dave were doing on 'Conversation Pieces', using the voices of ordinary people on a pre-recorded soundtrack. Rather than get other people to do all the sound recording, I did half of it myself. Also, instead of eavesdropping on the subjects, we interviewed them. In my mind I had the zoo theme planned out, so in the interviews I tried to ask questions that would produce the kind of answers that animals might make. I found a Brazilian student living in Bristol, so I asked him not only what he thought about zoos but also about the weather, the food and student accommodation. He said a surprising amount of things which fitted perfectly. Asked about the food in his hall of residence, he said, " ... and food that look more like dog food than food proper for wild animals. All right?"'

'He was so good that later I was able to let the soundtrack dictate to me what we should do when we filmed him as an animal. For some reason he kept mentioning double-glazing: "Here you have everything sorted out - double-glazing, your heating and everything, but you don't have *space*!" So I put a big glass window next to him to convey both the glazing and the fact that it helped to shut him in.

'Once we had recorded a voice, I tried to match it to a particular animal. People now say how well-suited the voices are to the animals, but in fact I changed things round a lot. At one point I thought the Brazilian could be a penguin rather than the Jaguar he became. My theory is that you can make anything fit anything. What is most important is how you do it.

'I found working with pre-recorded voices very refreshing. Although the format might seem rigid, and the filming process very straightforward, in fact it frees you up. Unlike a commercial, where you have to tell a complete story in thirty seconds, here you have time to let the voice give you ideas about how to animate and play with the character, all within the discipline of a static, held frame. To me this was liberating and very enjoyable to do.'

Each of the captive animals has a different view of what it is like to live in a zoo. Clockwise, from top left: The anxious but not unhappy Bush Baby - 'I know, whatever happens, they'll look after me'; Andrew the young Polar Bear, who takes a precociously global view of things; the Terrapins, reasonably comfortable but 'I can't actually get out and about'; the Armadillos, contented in a downtrodden sort of way; the young Hippopotamus who thinks that most of the cages are a bit small, and the philosophical Gorilla. Below: The spokesperson for the Birds, who reasons that animals in the zoo are better off than animals in the circus because 'they can do their own thing'.

Characterisation - Wallace and Gromit

Nick Park has won two Oscars and one nomination for his films featuring Wallace the inventor and Gromit, his dog. In chronological order they are *A Grand Day Out*, *The Wrong Trousers* and *A Close Shave*. Here, he describes how Wallace and Gromit came into being and how they have changed during the making of the three films.

'I sketched out my ideas for the characters way back in art school in Sheffield. I resurrected them at film school, and then I had this other idea about somebody - I did not know who - building a rocket in his basement and going to the Moon. I went back to the earlier characters to see if they could build the rocket. Gromit was then a cat, and I changed him into a dog. A dog would be chunkier and larger, and easier to work with in clay. I wrote a script, but this also changed a great deal once we started shooting. Some of the restrictions of working with clay started to dictate their characters.

'For example, Gromit originally had a voice, which we actually recorded. He was also going to leap about a lot and do tricks. At first I did not realise how difficult that would be to animate, but when we came to shoot the first scene I began to rethink the whole character. In this scene Wallace is sawing a door and Gromit is standing underneath acting as a trestle (see page 76). Because he was stuck under there, all I could move was his head, ears and eyebrows. So I did that, and then I saw I could get such a lot of character from just those little movements. This showed me that he did not need a stuck-on mouth as well, so we dropped the whole idea of Gromit speaking. It made a better contrast too, with Gromit now the quieter, more introverted character and Wallace the louder, more outgoing one.

'I find you can always make economy work for you, even if this is not at first apparent. For instance, it can be harder not to move something than it is to move it. Suppose you are shooting a character with a tail, and now it is eight hours since you last moved it. In film-time this may be only two seconds, but you can still get very impatient because you have not moved it. You have to watch this, otherwise your tail will be wiggling about the whole time and distracting the audience from the main character.

'As for the relationship between the two characters, this is still evolving. I am not one of those people who feels he has to know everything about his characters before shooting. People ask me questions like "What would Wallace buy Gromit for Christmas?" This is something I have never thought about, so I do not know the answer. I have not got there yet. I almost feel that they have their own life, so really I would have to ask them about it.'

Early sketches by Nick Park of Wallace and (a very different) Gromit.

Wallace and Gromit - an unlikely but unbeatable combination. Wallace the loud one, the man in command, the eccentric inventor whose machines are never totally under control. Gromit, quiet, dependable, with much more sense than his master.

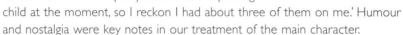

War Story

An old man recounts his memories of the Second World War - under the bombs in Bristol, when the cupboard under the stairs doubled as a coalhouse and an air-raid shelter - 'I sits on the coal, then in comes 'er mother and sits on my lap, and my missus sits on 'er mother's lap. My missus was expecting a child at the moment, so I reckon I had about three of them on me.' Humour and nostalgia were key notes in our treatment of the main character.

After 'Conversation Pieces', Channel 4 commissioned a similar series which we called 'Lip Synch'. We took the opportunity to try out new directors and new styles. In *War Story*, we abandoned the formula of recording conversations, and went instead for a recorded interview. We talked to Peter Lawrence of Radio Bristol, and he recommended this guy, Bill Perry, then probably in his seventies. Bill was a great raconteur, and Peter had interviewed him several times for radio. As usual, we decided not to meet him because we preferred to work in a state of innocence, so we asked Peter to do the interview, and he came back with two and a half hours of tape.

At the time I was quite tempted to do a serious piece, concentrating on the darker side of Bill's war memories. He had worked at the BAC aircraft factory

Images from the Home Front in the 1940s - a propeller aircraft at the BAC aircraft factory, Bristol, and the coalman emptying his sacks into the cupboard under the stairs.

on the outskirts of Bristol when it was bombed, and I thought I could make a faintly mournful, regretful film based on this side of his story. But, at about that time, I'd finished another film in the series, called *Going Equipped.* This was a serious piece about a petty criminal and the awful barren life he falls into. I liked the film, and still do, but simply because it did not have any laughs in it, people had been unsure how to react. This made me decide to go for a more light-hearted take on the material we had for *War Story.*

There was plenty of material to choose from, so we selected the bits we liked and tried to arrange them in a coherent order. One of the attractions was being able to mix scenes of the old man telling his stories in the present with others showing him acting them out as a younger man. The most difficult part was the ending. Bill had a lot of stories, but he never got to a really white-hot punchline with any of them. Fortunately, while describing the after-effects of sitting on a heap of coal with the other members of his family piled on top of him, he says, 'It was agony, Ivy, I was tattooed all over," which I believe is an old radio catch-phrase. Then I had him clamp his pipe firmly between his teeth with a loud "click", rather like Eric Morecambe used to do, waggle his eyebrows - and that was it. That was our ending. Not the world's best, perhaps, but it is quite a good example of how to bring your film to a pleasing end when the action or dialogue does not provide you with an obvious choice.

A happy ending - simply achieved with a click of National Health teeth on pipe, a grin and a quick waggle of the eyebrows.

Three characters in search of showbiz success - timorous Tiny, the dog-juggling music-hall star, devious Daphne and ruthless Arnold, full of cunning and frustrated rage. The story of their conflicts had to be put across in only eleven minutes, so every gesture and movement had to carry a special meaning.

Characterisation - *Stage Fright*

The story relates the sad decline of Tiny, the hero, from his days as a dog-juggling music-hall star to the present day. He is persecuted at every turn by Arnold, a manipulative bully, and although he receives occasional solace from Daphne, who says she will stick by him, she has her own interests very much at heart. Steve Box, the film's director, explains how he developed his characters.

'I get the motivation for my characters from the script. I had been thinking about the story for about two years, then I wrote *Stage Fright* over an intensive six-month period. This gave me a much better idea of the characters and how they would act in the film. I think most of us in animation do it this way round, rather than making a funny-looking model and then wondering what to do with it.

'Characters are really defined by the film they are in. I cannot imagine the characters of *Stage Fright* being in anything else; they are in their own world. The main theme is ambition, and the story shows the trials and tribulations of people who try to make their living as performers - and also dream of stardom or at least, in Arnold's case, enough money to help him forget his mediocrity. The film portrays a lot of negative emotions and the mood is fairly dark. All three characters want to succeed in show business, but none of them goes about it in the right way.

'Tiny is a casualty of trends in entertainment. His art is constantly being rejected and he becomes very reclusive, trapped in a decaying theatre and himself deteriorating as the building around him falls to bits. I made this come out in his appearance and gestures. He is often hunched and very short, only about half the size of Arnold who towers over him. While Tiny trembles, his arms raised in fear, Arnold is full of frustrated rage at his own lack of talent, and to match his violent behaviour he has alarming jagged hair and fierce teeth.

'Daphne is ambitious too. From the way they talk, it seems she and Tiny once worked together as performers, but then she double-crossed him to get her feet under the table with Arnold, seeing him as her ticket to a career in the silent movies. Actually, I think she is quite a nasty piece of work, with her big blue hair and lovely silk dress with bows on it - very artificial, and superficial too.

'Although the film lasts for only eleven minutes, the animation process allows you to get in a ton of information and suggestions about the characters. There is not time to show everything, but you can drop a lot of hints with something as small as a single gesture. Ours is a very condensed kind of film-making.'

Characterisation - Rex the Runt

Rex is the leader of a gang of four dogs who look more like gingerbread people with doggy ears. They live together, go on fantastic adventures, and are the conception of Richard Goleszowski, who explains how he sees them.

'I wanted the atmosphere of a flat-share between four characters in their early twenties, in that stage after college and before marriage. They all have their own identities and special quirks, but I try not to make them too predictable or type-cast, as you get in a traditional sitcom. I also like the fact that they can have childish, pastry cut-out figures and well-formed personalities at the same time. Rex is the self-appointed leader, which occasionally annoys the others. Bad Bob, who wears an eye patch and carries a gun, might seem to be a stereotype villain but he is not; this is just the way he looks. Wendy is Rex's part-time love interest, though both can get jealous if one of them fancies someone else. The fourth character, Vince, is either a complete idiot or a genius.

'No matter how surreal the adventure - voyaging through Vince's body in a submarine or deflating their own planet - there is always a contrast between the weird things they do and what they talk about. Their worries always come back to the most ordinary everyday things such as "Did you turn the iron off?"

'Unlike most puppets, Rex and his mates have flattened bodies, though the world around them is more or less normal. Having two-dimensional characters existing in a three-dimensional space allows us to produce reasonably good animation without having to deal with all the problems of gravity. We shoot the scenes both in conventional 3-D sets and with the characters placed on an

Front row, left to right: Rex, Vince. Back row: Bad Bob, Wendy.

Rex and friends in *Adventures on Telly Part Three,* in which the gang stumble on a branch of Poultry Pantry, the interstellar fast-food chain.

angled sheet of glass, behind which we can put photographic backgrounds or add live action using the green-screen process. This makes for quicker and cheaper shooting. In the process we make a lot of collages, and these help to bring the characters more into contact with the human world. This way you can have a nice multi-media shot of, say, plasticine dogs in a toy car weaving about in traffic on a real, filmed motorway.

'To me Rex the Runt is first of all a comedy show. The fact that we do it by animation is not the biggest part of it. We work quickly on several sets and I leave the animators space to make decisions about what props should look like and what a character is going to do. Although the results may sometimes be a little rough at the edges, I do not mind that. We get a lot of continuity mistakes as well, but I also think they are quite funny and encourage them. Big Bob's eye patch can jump from one eye to the other in the same scene, but no-one seems to notice. To me that is fun; a happy accident. What matters is that the films have humour, pace and energy - like a good comedy show.'

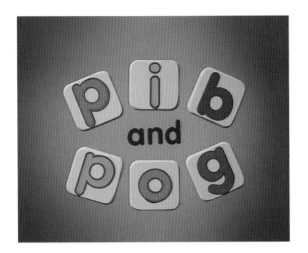

Characterisation - Pib and Pog

This film is a highly knockabout version of a children's TV show. It features two bulbous characters, Pib and Pog, who do increasingly violent and nasty things to each other, and the slightly nannyish voice of the female presenter, who mostly pretends that everything is all right really. She is never seen. At the end, Pib and Pog are revealed as two old luvvie actors who probably perform these hooligan roles on a regular basis. The film was written and directed by Peter Peake, who describes his approach.

'I saw Pib and Pog as a couple of animated characters playing a part and giving the cameras what they want to see, which is a very stylised kind of Tom and Jerry violence. As characters they are equals, each as bad as the other. Neither is prepared to back down, which is reason enough for the violence to escalate all the time, starting with childish squabbling and finishing with a cannon which they point at each other in mounting panic before it blows up and blasts the pair of them off the stage.

'In a way, Pib and Pog inflict violence on each other like Laurel and Hardy used to do. One of them just stands there and waits while the other one plots a new trick, then comes up and smacks him. There is a dreadful inevitability about what is going to happen next. It is certainly going to be violent; the only question in the audience's mind is what form it will take. One of my problems, in portraying this kind of inevitable violence, was to keep the interest going. I tried to do this not only by making each assault nastier than the one before, but also by devising unexpected bits as well, like the bed of nails which Pog rapidly produces while Pib is still gleefully bouncing up in the air after his latest triumph. Next moment, he is impaled and helpless, and the initiative has passed back to Pog.

'Against this grim war of attrition you have the voice of the patronising presenter who is continually telling the imaginary child audience what fun Pib and Pog are having. I think both these aspects are still true of children's television programmes, where you can see acts of quite horrific violence on film, the after-effects of which are quickly soothed away by a presenter who almost seems to have no idea about what the kids at home have really been watching.

Welcome to the cosy teatime world of Pib and Pog. 'Hello Pib, hello Pog,' cries the off-screen presenter. 'What have you been up to?'

Now let the mayhem begin. Oh look, Pog's head is jammed in a bucket. A moment later he emerges with his face missing. 'Why,' coos the presenter, 'it's concentrated sulphuric acid!'

Now Pib saws Pog in half. Pog responds by trapping Pib on a bed of nails. What fun they're having!

After the show, the actors say goodbye. 'What a dreadful ham,' says the Pog luvvie, after electrocuting his partner.

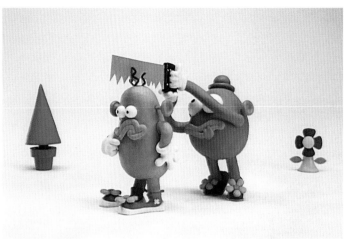

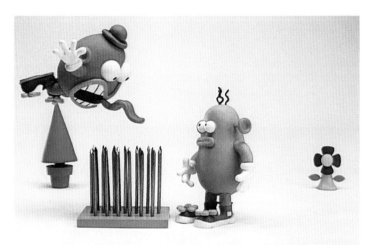

'There is a further jab at the cosy world of the TV studio when Pib and Pog fall back to earth again after the cannon blast and sing their cutesy little signature tune. As a final punchline, perhaps a reminder that violence is always around us, or at least an affirmation that the two actors are just as bad as the roles they play, the luvvies amble off-stage mouthing compliments to each other, then one electrocutes the other with his parting handshake.'

179

Editing

Helen Garrard has edited many films for Aardman. Here she explains her role.

'My first task on a film is to supervise the soundtrack. I am given a storyboard, and a script if there is dialogue in the film, and then I go to the dialogue recording. At Aardman, which is famous for its closely synchronised dialogue, we record the dialogue before any filming takes place. We come back with all the dialogue, choose the best takes and edit them down to a final version. It can be spaced out later, if necessary, but the essence of it is there. We then break down the dialogue phonetically and mark this on a series of charts. The animators work very closely to these when they match the movements of the characters to what they say. From the charts they can see the position of the mouth on each frame.

'While shooting is going on, the film is loosely edited in its longest form by the assistant editor, who sees the material as it arrives each day. When a sizeable chunk or scene is ready, I cut it together more closely, but still in quite a loose way so that, when we come to the final edit, we have still got plenty of flexibility with the footage.

'That is how we work with celluloid film. Methods are changing now with the new digital computerised editing system (AVID). When film is transferred on to one of the new machines, the editor has many more options to choose from. This is the way we will probably go in the future.

'Once the whole film has been shot, I sit with the director and we go through

Capturing the right mood for title-sequence lettering: a theatrical type for *Stage Fright*, and a rough-edged thriller style for *The Wrong Trousers*.

everything in detail. We trim it down, tighten it up, pace it, and maybe even move scenes around. This takes about two weeks for a 30-minute feature film. After that we start planning out the soundtrack in greater detail, including the sound effects and the music. Once the cut is complete, the composer can start composing to pictures.

'The various sounds are 'laid', in separate tracks. There may be a lot of them - on A Close Shave we had 26 tracks for the scenes with Preston after he has become a robot. While this is going on, we are also dealing with the optical houses who supply optical effects, titles and credit sequences. Then we pull everything together. We take all the soundtracks and the music into a special sound studio where they mix it all together and balance everything out. Then I send the lab a template on celluloid of the final cut (the 'cutting copy'), and they cut the negative according to that template. Once that is done, they produce a print that the lighting cameraman checks for colour balance, and from there we move to the final print.'

Sound

Adrian Rhodes is a specialist sound editor, or sound mixer. He has been responsible for the sound on a large number of live-action films as well as Aardman productions. Here he discusses his role.

'My job is to create sounds rather than to record them. I am not usually involved in the dialogue recording, but come in after about half the film has been shot and edited into a rough cut. At this stage I go through the material with the editor and the director, and then I can start to build up the sound effects that will be needed.

'Take the lorry in *A Close Shave*. In the beginning, I want to get the concept right, so I work on assembling appropriate lorry sounds that can be stretched or edited down later when filming is completed. I supply all the sounds needed in the film, not just the big ones like lorries or aircraft but also every footstep, rustle, or the noise that someone makes when they put their glasses down on a table. These little sounds are called foley or footstep sounds, and making them is specialised and highly skilled work. I work with a foley artist, who comes into the studio and acts out or makes up the sounds - walking along to the action pictures, for example, to provide the sound of footsteps. On the studio floor there is a panel of different surfaces - paving stone, floorboard, tarmac surface, etc. - which he can walk or run on to get the right sound.

At the mixing desk for the final mix, when all the sound components are brought together and balanced out.

'With animated films, one of the important things to remember is that real sounds, ie those directly imitated from life, can often seem out of place or unsuitable. If you want an exterior sound of tweeting birds, for example, it is probably not a good idea to record real birds in a garden. This is because the characters in the film are not real but clay creatures living in their own fantasy world, and so the sound of real tweeting birds may not sit well on the film. For the Penguin's feet in *The Wrong Trousers*, it would have been a mistake to record a real penguin flapping about. Instead, we got the foley artist to do it, and his solution was very simple: he just slapped his hands on his thighs to the rhythm of the walk.

'One of our most complex scenes, from the sound point of view, was in the cellar in *A Close Shave*, after Preston the dog had turned into a robot. The Preston sounds alone took up more than twenty different tracks, with different sound combinations for his head movements, feet, the roar, and so on. Also in that sequence there were several other elements - the conveyor belt, the machine that chews up the robot, the sheep, etc. What you can then do is focus on one particular element, building up the robot, for example, until you have got him working, and then you can mix all his separate tracks down to something more manageable, put them on one side and then focus on the sheep, and do the same for that character. This is what we call the premixing stage, where all the sounds are assembled and then mixed together so that, when we come to the final mix, all the sound components of the film have been reduced to the three strands of sound, dialogue and music. For the final mix we go into a big studio and all sit there together - the director, editor, sound editor and composer - and work through everything until we get the balance that we think is right.

'I would encourage anyone starting out to make films to try and get in as much sound as possible. Sound brings a film to life, and even the tiniest details can play a part in this, helping to make your film better and more believable.'

Music

Julian Nott composes music for film and television productions. He has written the music for several Aardman films, and here describes how he works.

'The composer can come in at various times, depending on the kind of film and the preferences of the director. In animated films, the music may be needed first if the film is dependent on a song which has to be written before anything else can be done. In more story-led films, I prefer to come in at the end when the editing is finished and I can write music to the pictures.

'This means you probably do not have much time, perhaps three or four weeks for a 30-minute Wallace and Gromit film, but at least I can be as certain as possible that the film will not be changed. If someone decides to change the cut, the composer often has to start work all over again. There is always the temptation to try desperately hard to change what you have already written to fit the new cut, but this never really works and so it means starting afresh.

183

'On most occasions I see rushes on a big screen, and when the film is finished I get a videotape to work from. At this time I have a meeting with the director, and he or she tells me what in general they are hoping to do with the music, and then we go through the film in more detail to decide where the cues should start and end.

'I take away the video, which has a time-code on it. This is a computer code which is on one of the audio channels of the tape. I can then lock all my computers and machines and instruments on to this time-code and write the music very specifically to each second of the film.

Julian Nott's sketch for the beginning of the motorbike chase in *A Close Shave*. Sketches such as this go to the orchestrator who works out the orchestration in detail and prepares the parts for the musicians.

'When I have written a certain amount, I demo it to the director. Nowadays we have a lot of technology to help us, and even at this stage we can demo an orchestral score, using synthesisers which can make an accurate representation of the real instrument. Once the composer gets the final OK, he really has to work fast. With an orchestral score there is not time for him to do the orchestration and the parts copying for all the members of the orchestra. On *A Close Shave*, for instance, we had some 65 musicians in the orchestra and about 25 cues. That means providing the musicians with 1625 sheets, all of which have to be written out for a particular instrument. To cope with this, I sketch out the music and bring in an orchestrator, and he does the detailed orchestration for me. When the parts come back, someone books a studio and arranges for the musicians to come in.

'Many film directors and producers feel quite overwhelmed when they hear the music being played for the first time against their pictures by a full orchestra. It is such a powerful sound. Once we are recording, it is very difficult for the director to make changes. In animated films, people do not have the kind of budget where you can waste time and keep 65 musicians hanging around while you change the music. When all the music is recorded, we mix it and then it goes off to be track-laid against the pictures. The composer may or may not be involved with this, but he will probably go to the final mix, where all the sounds and music are balanced and the film is then ready to go to the final print.'

A high-point from the motorbike chase in *A Close Shave*, which is accompanied by suitably heroic martial music.

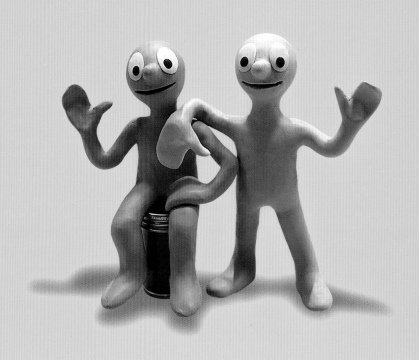

USEFUL INFORMATION

List of Suppliers

The following notes and addresses are intended as a general guide to the kind of suppliers who can help you with film-making equipment, rather than as a comprehensive list.
Check your Yellow Pages for further information, and look out for good modelmaking and art supply stores in your area.

Cameras

The best sources for 8mm and 16mm cine cameras are second-hand dealers or camera stores which have a second-hand cabinet. Always be sure the camera has a single-frame capacity. For video cameras, consult your local stockists for information on the latest developments in video cameras with an animation facility.

Camera Maker

Fries Engineering Inc
8743 Shirley Avenue
Northridge
California CA91324
tel 818 998 5400
fax 818 998 7553

Filmstock

Dr Rawstock (ALCP)
6916 Santa Monica Blvd, SLA
Hollywood
California CA90038
tel 310 441 4646
213 960 1781
fax 310 441 46 48

Film Stock Centre Blanx
70 Wardour St
London W1V 3HP
tel 0171 494 2244
fax 0171 287 2040

Fuji Photo Film (UK) Ltd
Fuji Film House
125 Finchley Road
London NW3 6JH
tel 0171 586 5900
fax 0171 722 4259

Fuji Photo Film (USA) Inc
555 Taxter Road, Elmsford
New York NY 10523
tel 201 5072500
fax 914 7898514

Ilford Imaging (UK) Ltd
Town Lane
Mobberley, Knutsford
Cheshire WA16 7JL
tel 01565 684000
fax 01565 873035

Iford Imaging Inc
West 70 Century Road
Paramus
New Jersey 07653
tel 201 2656000
fax 201 2650894

Kodak Ltd
Professional Motion Imaging
Station Rd, Hemel Hempstead
Herts HP1 1JU
tel 01442 261122
fax 01442 844458

Eastman Kodak Corporation
6700 Santa Monica Boulevard
PO Box 38939
Hollywood
California 90038-1203
tel 213 464 6131
fax 213 464 5886
www.kodak.com/go motion

and at:
360 W35th St
New York NY1001-2727
tel 212 631 3450
fax 212 631 3470

4 Concourse Parkway
Suite 300
Atlanta, Georgia 30328-5379
tel 770 522 6843
fax 770 522 6845

Oppenheimer Camera Inc
2645 N Mississippi Ave
Portland
Oregon Or 97227
tel 503 287 8666
fax 503 287 9165

Processing Laboratories

Background Engineers Inc
1133 Flower St
Glendale
California CA91201
tel 818 500 0454
818 432 0454
fax 818 500 8913C

Colour Film Services
10 Wadsworth Rd
Perivale, Greenford
Middlesex UB6 7JX
tel 0181 998 2731
fax 0181 997 8738

Cruse & Company Inc
7000 Romaine St
Hollywood
California CA90038
tel 213 851 8814

Metrocolor London Ltd
91-96 Gillespie Rd
London N5 1LS
tel 0171 226 4422
fax 0171 359 2353

Rank Film Laboratories
North Orbital Rd
Denham, Uxbridge
Middlesex UB9 5HQ
tel 01895 832323
fax 01895 832446

Soho Images
71 Dean St
London W1V 5HB
tel 0171 437 0831
fax 0171 734 9471

Technicolor Film Services Ltd
Bath Rd, West Drayton
Middlesex UB7 0DB
tel 0181 759 5432
fax 0181 799 6270

Todd-AO Filmatic
Horley Crescent
London NW1 8NT
tel 0171 284 7900
fax 0171 284 1018

Lighting and Sound Equipment

Stage Electrics Partnership Ltd
(incorporating SLX Ltd, Sound
Dept, Theatre Direct Ltd and
Theatre Vision Ltd) at:

Victoria Rd, Avonmouth
Bristol BS11 9DB
tel 0117 982 7282
fax 0117 982 2180

SLX Ltd
Victoria Rd, Avonmouth
Bristol BS11 9DB
tel 0117 982 6260
fax 0117 982 7778

Sound Dept
Blacklands Way
Abingdon Industrial Estate
Abingdon, Oxon OX14 1DY
tel 01235 555622
fax 01235 536654

Theatre Direct Ltd
Kirkwood Road
Kings Hedges
Cambridge CB4 2PH
tel 01223 423010
fax 01223 425010

Theatre Vision Ltd
Westpoint Industrial Estate
Penarth Rd, Cardiff CF1 7JQ
tel 01222 701212
fax 01222 701070

Action Lighting
46 Kansas Avenue
Salford, Manchester
M5 2GL
tel 0161 876 0576
fax 0161 876 0517

Hansard Vision
6056 W Jefferson Blvd
Los Angeles
California CA90016
tel 310 840 5660
818 780 2156
fax 310 840 5662

Introvision International Inc
1011 N Fuller Ave
Los Angeles
California CA90046
tel 213 851 9262
fax 213 851 1649

Christopher Nibley
Cinematography
12718 Valley Spring Lane
Studio City
California CA91604
tel 818 509 1613
fax 818 509 0625

Preferred Electrical
18 Lettice St, Fulham
London SW6 4EH
0171 731 0805
fax 0171 731 0623

Valiant Lamps
20 Lettice St, Fulham
London SW6 4EH
tel 0171 736 8115
fax 0171 731 3339

Modelmaking Equipment

This covers a broad area. The main components are modelling clays, silicones, foam latex, polyurethanes, resins, release agants, paints, inks, glues, metalwork and engineering supplies. Some of these can be obtained at local modelmaking and art supply stores. For some of the more specialist items we go to:

Armatures and ball-and-socket joints to order

John Wright Modelmaking
Workshop 1
Bristol Craft and Design Centre
6 Leonard Lane
Bristol BS1 1EA
tel/fax 0117 927 2854

Aluminium wire for simple armatures and prototypes

HC Rowland & Co
Rowland House
Delamere Rd, Cheshunt
Herts EN8 9SP
tel 01992 627377
fax 01992 628111

K & S Trade equipment

Chart international
Chart House, Station Road
East Preston, Littlehampton
West Sussex. BN16 5AG
tel 01903 773170
fax 01903 782152

Plasters and silicones

South Western Industrial Plasters
The Old Dairy
Hawk St, Bromham
Chippenham, Wilts SN15 2HU
tel 01380 850616

American modelling clay

Van Aken International
9157 Rochester Court
Rancho Cucamonga
California 91729
tel 909 980 2001
fax 909 980 2333

Filmography

KEY
Series titles in quotes
Film titles in italics
D/A = Direction/Animation
D = Direction
A = Animation
PA = Primary Animation

Short Films

1978

'Animated Conversations'
Confessions of a Foyer Girl
Down and Out
D/A Peter Lord & David
Sproxton, 5 min

1981-83

'The Amazing Adventures
of Morph'
26 episodes
D/A Peter Lord & David
Sproxton
5 min

'Conversation Pieces'
On Probation
Sales Pitch
Palmy Days
Early Bird
Late Edition
D/A Peter Lord & David
Sproxton, 5 min

1986

Babylon
D/A Peter Lord & David
Sproxton
14 min 30 sec

1989

'Lip Synch'
Next
D/A Barry Purves
Ident
D/A Richard Goleszowski
Going Equipped
D/A Peter Lord
Creature Comforts
D/A Nick Park
War Story
D/A Peter Lord,
5 min each

*A Grand Day Out**
D/A Nick Park, 23 min
*Produced by the National Film
& Television School and finished
with the help of Aardman
Animations

Lifting the Blues
D David Sproxton, 52 min

1990-91

*Rex the Runt - How Dinosaurs
Became Extinct*
D/A Richard Goleszowski, 2 min

1991

Rex the Runt - Dreams
D/A Richard Goleszowski, 2 min

Adam
D/A Peter Lord, 6 min

1992

Never Say Pink Furry Die
D/A Louise Spraggon, 12 min
Loves Me ... Loves Me Not
D/A Jeff Newitt, 8 min

1993

The Wrong Trousers
D Nick Park
A Nick Park & Steve Box, 29 min

Not Without My Handbag
D/A Boris Kossmehl, 12 min

1994

Pib & Pog
D/A Peter Peake, 6 min

1995

A Close Shave
D Nick Park
A Nick Park, Steve Box, Peter
Peake,
Lloyd Price, Gary Cureton,
Ian Whitlock, Sergio Delfino,
29 min

1996

Pop
D/A Sam Fell, 5 min

Wat's Pig
D Peter Lord
A Peter Lord, Sam Fell, Mike
Booth, 11 min

1997

Stage Fright
D Steve Box
A Steve Box, Jason Spencer-
Galsworthy,
Gary Cureton, Lloyd Price, Dave
Osmand, 11 min

Owzat
D/A Mark Brierley, 4 min 45 sec

1998

Hum Drum
D/A Peter Peake, 7 min

Al Dente
D/A Mark Brierley, 2 min

Angry Kid X3
D/A Darren Walsh, 1 min each

'Rex the Runt'
13 episodes
D Richard Goleszowski
A Sergio Delfino,
Dave Osmand,
Chris Sadler, Nick Upton,
Guest Frame Sam Fell
PA Grant White, 10 min

Pop Promos

1986

Sledgehammer
D Stephen Johnson
A Peter Lord, Nick Park,
Richard Goleszowski,
Brothers Quay,
4 min 30 sec approx

1987

Barefootin'
D/A Richard Goleszowski,
2 min 30 sec

My Baby Just Cares For Me
D/A Peter Lord, 3 min approx

1988

Harvest For The World
D/A (Aardman sequence)
David Sproxton, Peter Lord,
Richard Goleszowski, 4 min approx

1996

Never In Your Wildest Dreams
D Bill Mather
PA Paul Smith, Olly Reid,
Sergio Delfino, 3 min 57 sec

1998

Viva Forever
D Steve Box
A Steve Box, Darren Robbie,
Seamus Malone, 4 min 10 sec

Public Information Films

HIV/AIDS
D David Sproxton, Steve Box
A Steve Box

Commercials 1982 - 1998

Films completed for the following
clients/products:
Access, Ace Bars, Airwick,
American Express Travel, Angel
Delight, Ariston, Bitza Pizza,
Bonduelle, Bowyers Sausages,
Britannia Building Society, Burger
King, Cadbury's, Capri-Sun, Central
Office of Information, Chevron,
Chewits, Colgate, Compact
Games, Cook Electric, Crunchie,
Cuprinol, Daewoo, Dishwash
Electric, Domestos, Ducros,
Duracell, Duvivier, Electricity
Board, Enterprise Computers
Finches, Frisps, Gaymers Cider,
Grolsch, Guinness, Hamlet,
Hunters Crisps, Isseo, Jelmoli,
Jordans Crunchy Bars, KP, Kelloggs,
Laban Jellybabies, Lego, Les Autos,
Lipton, Little Caesars, London
Zoo, Lurpak, Lyles Golden Syrup
McVities Pizza, Manchester
Evening News, Maynards
Meccano, Meule d'Or, Mita, Nerds,
Nestlé, Oberlin, Perrier, Polo,
Purina Gravy, Quavers, Quickbrew
Rabobank, Ready-Brek, Rice
Krispies, Ruffles, SMC, St Ivel,
Savlon, Scotch Videotape, Scottish
Health Education Group, Shower
Electric, Smarties, Starburst, Tann's,
Terence Higgins Trust, Toppas, Total
Heating, Trimspoon, Tumbledry
Electric, Wagon Wheels, Walkers
French Fries, Weetabix, Weetos

Bibliography

Archer, Steve, *Willis O'Brien:
Special Effects Genius* (McFarland
& Co Inc, Jefferson, North
Carolina) 1993
Bendazzi, Giannalberto, *Cartoons:
One hundred years of cinema
animation* (John Libbey,
London) 1994
Canemaker, John, *Winsor McCay:
His Life and Art* (Abbeville Press
(New York, NY) 1987
Crafton, Donald, *Emile Cohl,
Caricature and Film* (Princeton
University Press, Princeton,
NJ) 1990
ibid, *Before Mickey: The Animated
Film, 1898-1928* (MIT Press,
Cambridge, Mass) 1982
Edera, Bruno & (ed) Halas, John,
Full Length Animated Feature Films
(Focal Press, London) 1977
Frierson, Michael, *Clay Animation:
American Highlights 1908 to the
Present* (Twayne Publishers /
Simon & Schuster Macmillan, New
York, NY) 1994
Halas, John, *Masters of Animation*
(BBC Books, London) 1987
Halas, John & Manvell, Roger, *The
Technique of Film Animation* (Focal
Press, London) 1968
Harryhausen, Ray, *Film Fantasy
Scrapbook* (Titan Books
London) 1989
Hickman, Gail Morgan, *The Films
of George Pal* (AS Barnes and Co
Inc, South Brunswick, NJ) 1977
Holliss, Richard & Sibley, Brian *The
Disney Studio Story* (Octopus,
London / Crown, New York,
NY) 1988
Holman, L Bruce, *Puppet
Animation in the Cinema* (AS
Barnes and Co Inc, South
Brunswick, NJ) 1975
Home, Anna, *Into the Box of
Delights: A History of Children's
Television* (BBC Books,
London) 1993
Horne, Maurice (ed), *The World
Encyclopedia of Cartoons* (Chelsea
House Publishers, New York,
NY) 1980
Martin, Leona Beatrice & Martin,
François, *Ladislas Starewitch* (JICA
Diffusion, Bibliography 2
Annecy) 1991
Pilling, Jayne (ed), *Starewich
1882-1965* (Film House,
Edinburgh) 1983
Robinson, David, *George Méliès:
Father of Film Fantasy* (Museum of
the Moving Image, London) 1993
Sibley, Brian (ed), *Wallace &
Gromit Storyboard Collection: A
Close Shave* (BBC Worldwide
Publishing Ltd, London) 1997
Thomas, Bob, *Walt Disney the Art
of Animation* (Golden Press, New
York, NY) 1958
Thompson, Frank, *Tim Burton's
Nightmare Before Christmas: The
Film, The Art, The Vision* (Hyperion,
New York, NY) 1993

Picture Acknowledgments

ACKNOWLEDGMENTS

Many thanks also to everyone at or connected with Aardman Animations who
in some way helped to make this book happen, especially:

Photography
Tristan Oliver, Dave Alex Riddett
Text Contributions
Tom Barnes, Steve Box, Mark Brierley, Trisha Budd, Debbie Casto,
Helen Garrard, Richard Goleszowski, Phil Lewis, Julian Nott,
Nick Park, Peter Peake, Adrian Rhodes, Dave Alex Riddett,
Jan Sanger, David Sproxton, John Wright
Special Photography

Photographer	Richard Laing
Art Director	Darren Walsh
Producer	Zoë Grimwood
Archive Stills/Footage/Artwork	Kieran Argo, Andrea Redfern, Maggie O'Connor
Animation	Peter Lord, Loyd Price, Darren Walsh, Seamus Malone
Modelmaking	Kevin Wright, Debbie Casto, Zennor Box,
	John Wright, Jeff Cliff, Will La Trobe-Bateman,
	Mr Jones the Glassmaker
Modelmaking Coordination	Kerry Evans, Jan Sanger, Chris Entwhistle
Set Design	Phil Lewis
Director of Photography	Dave Alex Riddett
Sparks	John Truckle
Rigger	Nick Upton
Additional Artwork	Darren Walsh
Special Thanks	Liz Keynes, Jo Allen, Mike Cooper, Arthur Sheriff,
	Michael Rose, Alison Cook

A Sears Pocknell book	
Editorial Direction	Roger Sears
Art Direction	David Pocknell
Editor	Michael Leitch
Designers	Jonathan Allan and Bob Slater

Library of Congress Cataloging-in-Publication Data
Lord, Peter.
Creating 3-D animation : the Aardman book of filmmaking / by Peter Lord
and Brian Sibley ; foreword by Nick Park.
p.   cm.
Includes bibliographical references and index.
ISBN 0-8109-1996-6 (hardcover)
1. Animation (Cinematography). 2. Three-dimensional display
systems. 3. Aardman Animations (Firm) I. Sibley, Brian.
II. Aardman Animations (Firm) III. Title.
TR897.5.L67 1998
778.5' 347—dc21   98-16923

Published in Great Britain under the title
Cracking Animation: The Aardman Book of 3-D Animation
Printed and bound in Singapore by Imago

Harry N. Abrams, Inc.
100 Fifth Avenue
New York, N.Y. 10011
www.abramsbooks.com

192